W9-DES-427

COACHING SOCCER
THE
PROGRESSIVE WAY

COACHING SOCCER THE PROGRESSIVE WAY

Mike Ditchfield
and
Walter Bahr

PRENTICE HALL
Englewood Cliffs, New Jersey 07632

Prentice-Hall International (UK) Limited, *London*
Prentice-Hall of Australia Pty. Limited, *Sydney*
Prentice-Hall Canada, Inc., *Toronto*
Prentice-Hall Hispanoamericana, S.A., *Mexico*
Prentice-Hall of India Private Limited, *New Delhi*
Prentice-Hall of Japan, Inc., *Tokyo*
Simon & Schuster Asia Pte. Ltd., *Singapore*
Editora Prentice-Hall do Brasil, Ltda., *Rio de Janeiro*

© 1988 *by*
PRENTICE-HALL, INC.
Englewood Cliffs, NJ

10   9   8   7   6   5   4   3   2   1

Library of Congress Cataloging-in-Publication Data

Ditchfield, Mike.
  Coaching soccer the progressive way.

  Includes index.
  1. Soccer—Coaching.   I. Bahr, Walter.   II. Title.
GV943.8.D58   1988   796.334'07'7   87-36116
ISBN 0-13-139262-X
ISBN 0-13-139288-3 (pbk.)

Printed in the United States of America

ISBN 0-13-139262-X

ISBN 0-13-139288-3 {PBK}

PRENTICE HALL
BUSINESS & PROFESSIONAL DIVISION
A division of Simon & Schuster
Englewood Cliffs, New Jersey 07632

DEDICATION

This book is dedicated to the special people in my life.
To my Mother and Father, who so lovingly brought me into this life.
To my sister Susan and her family, who helped build my life.
To Walter Bahr, a man with no equal who gave sense to my life.
To David Clements, a coach who gave purpose to my life.
To Gordon Miller, a friend who believed in my life.
To Kathleen who showed me that there is more to life.
To Liam, who trusted me in life.
To all the children who became my life.

—Mike Ditchfield

"Sooner or later we run into situations too big for us to handle. In
real life we can avoid them, in sport we cannot, and that
leads us to the most remarkable self-discovery."

—Source Unknown

ACKNOWLEDGMENTS

It has often been said that a journey of a thousand miles begins with the first step. Six years after conceiving the idea and taking that first step, the journey is now complete. Of all the sights and sounds that I have encountered, it is the people along this journey that have inspired me and allowed me to dare to dream. It was with them that the future began. I feel honored that I can include them in print even though their true worth extends far beyond the covers of this book.

The Barringer Family
The Bahr Family
Edward Keynes
John Lucas
The Bressie Family
Buck and Cindy Scott
Doug Wead, Dexter Yeager and Ed Kinnet
The Maierhofer Family
Don Bevis
Duncan MacEwan
Lisa Hart
Michael Miller, Frank Little, Donald Levy
The Penn State Athletic Department
The Penn State Physical Education Department
The Penn State Soccer Team
Artwork—Barbara Hendrickson
Photographs—Steve Sanders

—Mike Ditchfield

HOW THIS BOOK CAN HELP YOU

Coaching Soccer the Progressive Way is not just another coaching book on soccer. We are beyond the stage of listing the rules of the game or explaining what a soccer uniform consists of. Instead we must extend ourselves as coaches to teaching the game in a manner that is simple, realistic, and understandable. It is often difficult to derive any sense out of what some coaching books are attempting to get across to the reader. This is never more evident than when confronted with diagrammed drills where the prerequisite to understanding is a degree in geometry.

Acquiring knowledge while coaching is a necessity, but of equal importance is the communication of this knowledge to the players. The first section of this book introduces a simplified technique to effective coaching. There are many books concerned with the art and science of coaching, stating facts that have been proven with research in this field. The problem is, however, that often the facts cannot be retained by coaches because issues are presented in so much detail there is not enough time to absorb all the information. In Section One we have concerned ourselves with three areas of effective coaching that are both informative and easy to implement.

The remainder of the book is concerned with the concept of teaching through the *Ripple Approach*. This approach takes on meaning through terminology made simple using a *Numbers-to-Action* system. In clear, understandable steps this system explains and illustrates **Positionless Soccer,** with its rotating positions and mass involvement of players that allow each player to experience different functions at different times and in different areas of the field. Teaching all players all positions adds to the understanding of the total game.

We firmly believe that you will derive satisfaction and success from being able to build the game into its understandable parts using this fresh and innovative approach to coaching. We wish you the success and accomplishment that go along with hard work and dedication. In beginning or continuing your personal coaching style, give some thought to becoming open to different ideas. The extent of your success depends on you, not only to the extent of the effort you give but also to the extent of your receptiveness toward change. The mind, like a parachute, works only when it's open.

—Mike Ditchfield and Walter Bahr

CONTENTS

SECTION ONE

Progressive Soccer
Technique

CHAPTER 1

Elements of Effective Coaching

PREPARATION

Successful performance in the game of soccer is directly linked to the motivational level of the players and the coach. Motivational factors are as important in the development of a player in his early stages as they are in maintaining his skill level in the future.

Players need to have their skills challenged at every opportunity provided these challenges are carefully planned. When you are preparing for and conducting a coaching session, pay attention to two areas:

Self-Preparation	The Coach
Group Preparation	The Team

Self-Preparation

You should be aware that your coaching session actually begins before coming into contact with players. Plan the session as thoroughly as possible, so as to limit errors that will only hinder you further once the session begins. It is helpful to check the following:

- *How many players are involved?* This means simply being aware of whether the working space will be suitable for the technique or skill that is to be carried out. By using the most suitable space, your players will not waste valuable time adjusting to an unrealistic environment. For example, if you are working on the topic of "creating space," there is little benefit in trying to work in a large area with a small group. By doing this you have already created the space, with practically no effort from the players.

- *What kind of equipment will be needed?* The more soccer balls you have available the more beneficial it will be for teaching techniques such as individual ball control, shooting, or goalkeeping. For younger children, look closely at the possibilities of using a smaller ball with smaller goals on a scaled-down field. A sandbox is an ideal setting for a goalkeeper to work in as it reduces many of the injuries that can arise from diving on a hard surface. Different-colored bibs are essential in order to quickly identify different groups or teams during practice. Using this system provides a readily observable, total picture of the game. Cones can be used for marking distances as well as for setting up goals and target areas.

- *Would I find it easier to use a coaching grid?* A coaching grid is made up of a series of 10-yard x 10-yard squares that act as a controlled environment for learning. The number of grids used will be determined by what is being taught. (Use cones to mark off the grids if lines cannot be painted on the field.) Grids provide an area where players can identify with their tasks and territory. The coaching grid is by no means the solution to all coaching problems, but it is probably the most significant coaching aid in soccer today. See Diagrams 1-1 and 1-2.

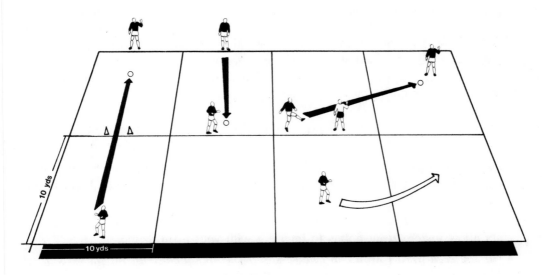

DIAGRAM 1-1
THE COACHING GRID

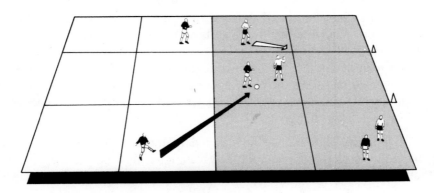

DIAGRAM 1-2
OFFENSE VERSUS DEFENSE IN THE GRID

Group Preparation

- *Where is the best coaching position to make sure the group can see and hear me?* This will depend on many factors including the number of players involved, the technique or skill being practiced, the position of the sun, and whether or not there are any distracting noises. With a smaller group of players you can become more involved with the individual player than you can when working with a larger group.

  If there is a distraction try to make the best of the situation. Face the sun, especially if you are demonstrating, so the players can get a clear picture without having to deal with bright sunlight. Work the practice as far from traffic and other activities as possible, so you can be heard and have the full attention of your players.

- *Is there a start and finish to the practice?* The start of a practice can take different forms as can the finish. You can use the start to warm players up through stretching and running or even playing small-sided games. Regardless of the activity chosen, this time should be used as a motivational period for the group.

  The finish of a practice is normally the time when you would emphasize and reinforce the major points of your session.

OBSERVATION

- *Do I know what I am looking for during the practice?* If you do not know or if what you are looking for does not appear, then the chances are that the initial preparation is at fault.

- *Am I watching the ball or around the ball?* Be single-minded about the topic and do not allow insignificant points to interfere with your main theme.

- *Having seen what I want can I make sure I keep the picture for the player's benefit?* This is crucial as it removes any artificial setting up of a situation. You should work at maintaining realism throughout the practice. Do not attempt to stop play after the incident has passed in the hope of trying to re-create it. It is more appropriate to allow play to continue without stopping until another incident occurs.

- *Is there a breakdown in the player's technique or skill?* Keep in mind the difference between technique and skill: technique is *how* to perform a certain physical action with the ball in isolation; skill is *when* and *where* to perform the technique in the game situation. Knowing how to shoot is a technique; knowing when and where to shoot is a skill.

  To develop technique the practice requires a ball. To develop skill the practice requires *opposition,* since there are opponents in the game; *teammates,* since in the game players must cooperate with each other; and *targets,* since all practice must lead toward or away from the goal.

Though a practice session may be devoted to the repetition of an individual ball technique, the successful performance of that technique must not be the objective of the practice. Individual techniques are part of a tactical plan and should be viewed as such. Technical superiority, by way of more refined ball play techniques, will not automatically ensure overall tactical success. This is not to undervalue the importance of individual ball techniques, but to emphasize that they are only a small part of the tactical objectives. Players should learn how to apply themselves to the ball and for what purposes. Decision making is an important part of soccer skill. To be able to pass a ball the first time is one thing; knowing when to do that rather than to control the ball is another.

INSTRUCTION

- *Do the players understand what is wanted?* Players can follow instructions only if they first, understand what is required and second, see a need for it. You should verbally and visually create a situation easily interpreted by players if any positive coaching and learning is to take place.

- *Can I communicate with the players?* Demonstrations are usually accompanied by verbal explanation; therefore, it is important to be able to communicate something of value. Misunderstanding often results from a misused vocabulary. Attempt to avoid jargon and speak clearly and concisely.

- *How do I coach in the game situation?*
  - –Freeze Work: Here the practice game is stopped so you can instruct the players. Players must realize that they are to freeze immediately in their positions. This method is particularly effective when you are introducing new tactics.

  - –Condition Work: When a particular aspect of game play needs to be stressed, impose an artificial condition on your players. This condition is a restriction that will make a more frequent demand on that aspect of play. Some conditions produce unrealistic play; therefore, you should impose such restrictions only for a short period of time.

  - –Directing Play: Verbal instructions are given to the players during play without actually stopping the game. This method can be effective provided that the players do not rely totally on your instructions.

Thorough preparation produces clearer observation and more relevant instruction.

SECTION
TWO

Progressive Soccer

Theory

CHAPTER 2

Progressive Coaching

This chapter sets forth a step-by-step procedure designed for your needs in planning and implementing different areas of progressive coaching.

CHOOSING A PLAYING POSITION

The Ripple Approach

A stone that is thrown into water has the effect of creating ripples, the stone being the source of these ripples. In soccer, the ball represents this stone and the players represent the ripples. Everything is centered around the ball. Coaching begins in this immediate area and deals first with the player who is in possession of the ball. This player is referred to as:

- 1st Man Offense

The coaching of all techniques and skills concerned with the ball will be discussed under this heading later in this book. These techniques and skills are:

–Controlling: This should be taught early or there will be little foundation on which to build anything else in a player's development.

–Shooting: This should be the primary choice of a player. There are occasions when this action is unrealistic but players have to be encouraged to accept responsibility.

–Passing: This second choice should be made when a shot cannot be taken. Successful passing allows a team to retain possession of the ball.

–Dribbling: Younger players have a tendency to make this their first choice, which in turn leads to a swarming around the ball. It can very often lead to a loss of possession; therefore, it should be the third choice for a player.

–Heading: Balls that are in the air can also be played in the air if a player is competent in this skill.

It is an accepted fact that players must concern themselves with making the correct decision in choosing one skill over another. The main concern for you is to place these skills in a semblance of order.

The player on defense who is directly opposing the threat from the ball is:

- 1st Man Defense

This area of defense is probably the most significant as it concerns destroying the main point of attack.

In moving out and away from the ball the next ripple introduces two more players and their respective roles. The player offering immediate support to the 1st Man Offense is referred to as the:

- 2nd Man Offense

The player who indirectly opposes this player and who is offering immediate support to the 1st Man Defense is referred to as the:

- 2nd Man Defense

In moving away even further from the ball you are now dealing with the most difficult area of soccer. This area includes every other player on the field, both offense and defense. The players who are on offense attempt to create and use space. They will be referred to as the:

- 3rd Man Offense

The players who are on defense attempt to deny space. They will be referred to as the:

- 3rd Man Defense

The Ripple Approach will become more meaningful when stress is placed on the continual reinforcement of certain points to certain players at certain times. The terminology that will be used in the Ripple Approach is limited in part to numbers. You are working from a Numbers-to-Action system.

Diagram 2-1 presents an overall view of the steps involved in coaching soccer the progressive way. Diagram 2-2 illustrates the ripple approach to playing positions.

CHOOSING A COACHING LEVEL

After having decided the playing position to be worked on, there is a need to know at what level you should direct your drills and scrimmages. How do you adapt the drills to the different technique and skill levels found in your players?

The more proficient player will need to work under more pressure than the player who is learning the fundamentals. The starting point is to make a basic assumption that practice is a necessary component in the acquisition of soccer skill. The arguments against practice are not so much raised against the need for it, as against the nature of it.

Some techniques and skills, usually the basic ones such as control with the thigh, can be acquired by practicing them as a complete action. Others are too complicated, and are best broken down into more understandable segments. The whole game of soccer must be

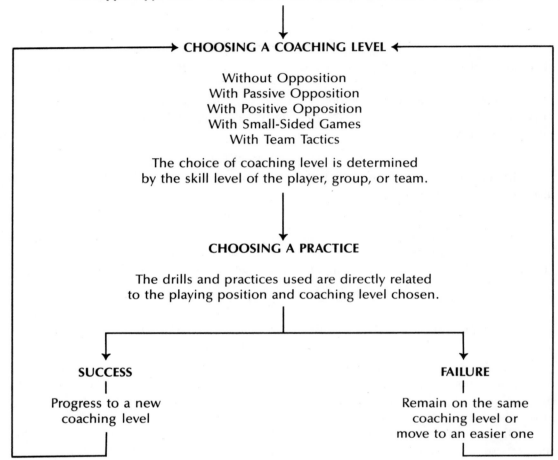

CHOOSING A PLAYING POSITION
The Ripple Approach—1st, 2nd, 3rd Man Offense & Defense. Goalkeeper.

CHOOSING A COACHING LEVEL

Without Opposition
With Passive Opposition
With Positive Opposition
With Small-Sided Games
With Team Tactics

The choice of coaching level is determined
by the skill level of the player, group, or team.

CHOOSING A PRACTICE

The drills and practices used are directly related
to the playing position and coaching level chosen.

SUCCESS

Progress to a new
coaching level

FAILURE

Remain on the same
coaching level or
move to an easier one

DIAGRAM 2-1
COACHING SOCCER THE PROGRESSIVE WAY

broken down into more understandable parts. Fortunately these parts can themselves be interesting and are easily reassembled into a complete game.

The game of soccer for young players need not, indeed should not, be the adult form of soccer with eleven players on each side. This is far too sophisticated a concept for all but the most mature ten- and eleven-year-olds. Most young players will better comprehend a game involving smaller numbers of players on a smaller field, with smaller goals and a smaller ball.

The main purpose of the drills and small-sided games is to allow the players to be active in a stimulating and realistic situation, in which they are successful and which can be related at all times to a game setting they can also understand. The following diagram exhibits the

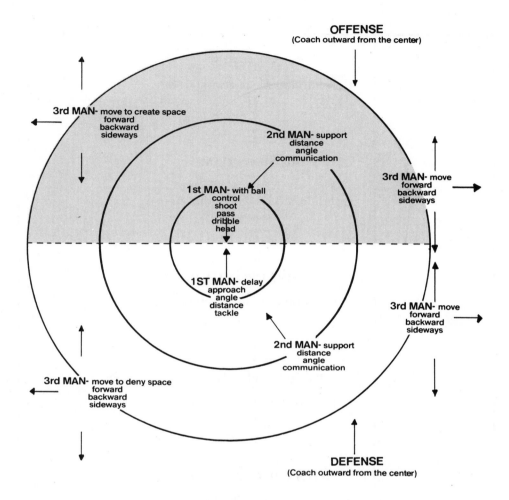

OFFENSE
(Coach outward from the center)

3rd MAN- move to create space
forward
backward
sideways

2nd MAN- support
distance
angle
communication

3rd MAN- move
forward
backward
sideways

1st MAN- with ball
control
shoot
pass
dribble
head

1ST MAN- delay
approach
angle
distance
tackle

2nd MAN- support
distance
angle
communication

3rd MAN- move
forward
backward
sideways

3rd MAN- move to deny space
forward
backward
sideways

DEFENSE
(Coach outward from the center)

DIAGRAM 2-2
CHOOSING A PLAYING POSITION
THE RIPPLE APPROACH

hierarchy directly related to choosing a coaching level. (See Diagram 2-3.) The choice of coaching level is determined by the technique or skill level of the individual or team. Throughout the learning phase of a player's development, he or she should move up through the different coaching levels. For example, a player who has never controlled a ball with his chest will work Without Opposition while he is learning the basics of this technique.

In the stage of a player performing a skill, the coach will move down through the coaching levels, until a level is found that can be worked at. Professional teams will work extensively at the Team Tactics level because the majority of breakdowns occur at this level during the game. Diagram 2-3 illustrates the levels just discussed.

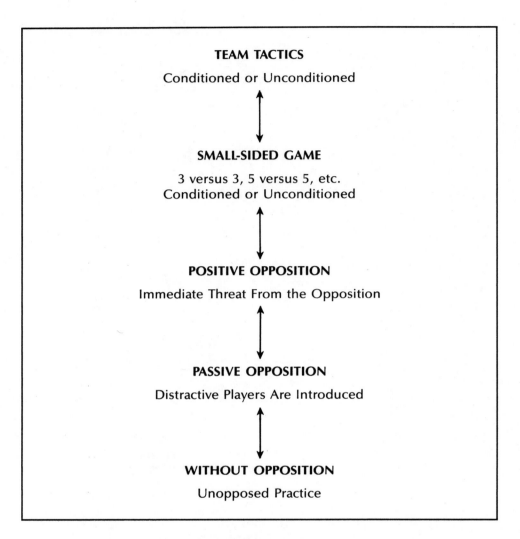

DIAGRAM 2-3
CHOOSING A COACHING LEVEL

Without Opposition

At this level the various factors in the game are gradually introduced without the presence of any obstacles, which at this stage may hinder the learning process. When working without opposition, the level of instruction is very basic. It is at this level that the purest form of technique is taught. A certain amount of decision making is required, but the extent of it is limited, as players will comprehend only a small amount of information. (See Diagram 2-4.)

DIAGRAM 2-4
WITHOUT OPPOSITION

Players passing in pairs in a 10-yard x 10-yard coaching grid. The ball is passed in a straight line on the ground, with the inside of the foot. The ball must be controlled before it can be passed. The players must attempt 10 passes.

With Passive Opposition

It is at this level that the coach moves closer to a skill situation. A passive opponent is introduced who takes little part in the drill. His presence merely acts as a distraction to the other players. The passive opponent has one major role and that is to give the other players more to concentrate on, without actually making any physical contact. This will normally take the form of a distracting movement across the intended path of the ball or toward the player in possession of the ball. (See Diagram 2-5.)

DIAGRAM 2-5
PASSIVE OPPOSITION

A third player is introduced who runs across the intended path of the ball as it is passed across the grid. The more proficient the player becomes in passing, the closer this third player will run in front of him.

With Positive Opposition

The effectiveness of the opposition is gradually increased, until the skill can be performed in a realistic situation. Working time and working space begin to play a much more important role at this level, as decisions have to be made quickly in an effort to maintain possession. This coaching level becomes the stage whereby players are introduced into the different functions and phases of the game. There must be opportunities for players to involve themselves with an immediate threat from defenders. Only with this type of realistic game situation will the level of playing performance improve. (See Diagram 2-6.)

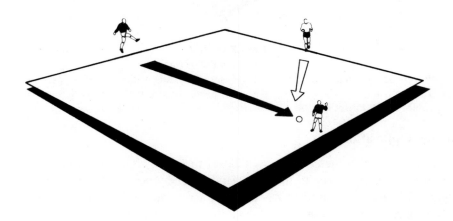

DIAGRAM 2-6
POSITIVE OPPOSITION
The third player now runs from a side of the grid to offer a challenge. If the pass is continually successful, then it becomes evident that the player under pressure can perform the skill soundly. He knows *when* and *where* to pass and not just *how* to pass. The player receiving the pass back from the player under pressure can move from side to side, in an effort to force the player passing to look up first.

Small-Sided Game

In this situation the skill of passing the ball is made that much more difficult by the presence of positive opposition and supporting teammates. The player with the ball is hindered not only by one player from the opposition, but by other players as well. His teammates are going to offer some assistance, but decisions have to be made as to which teammate is the most helpful.

As the practice becomes more game-like, skill becomes more difficult to perform. A small-sided game should be used to emphasize the skill being taught. Do not overload players with too much information, which is irrelevant to the skill being covered. Conditions can be imposed at this level to reinforce major coaching points. (See Diagram 2-7.)

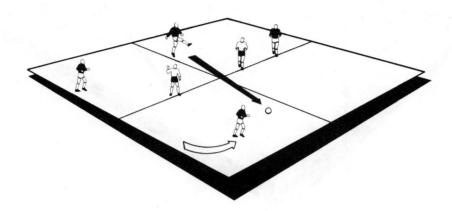

DIAGRAM 2-7
SMALL-SIDED GAME

Having created a 4 vs. 2 situation in four grids, the aim is for the offensive players to work the ball around, until it can be passed between the two defenders to an open player. This pass is often referred to as "splitting the defense." Once this has been mastered, other defenders can be added. Goals can be introduced to bring out direction and targets.

Team Tactics

This is an extension of the small-sided game, which moves the play into a more realistic setting. All skills are performed with one major objective in mind, that of re-creating these skills in a game situation. The tactics stage of coaching will undoubtedly depend upon the progress of the players.

Small-sided games can be used extensively to highlight areas of the game, but eventually all previous learning has to be integrated into the environment of a full-sided game. The 3rd Man Offense and 3rd Man Defense now play a more prominent role in what is being coached. It can be a difficult stage of coaching and learning, but if the build-up in the previous stages has been well-organized and instructed, then a team situation need not be too confusing. Individual performance in combination play is a major concern in any aspect of team tactics.

The team tactic level does not always have to be comprised of an 11 vs. 11 game. Tactical units will begin to form around the ball, with certain intentions in mind. Tactical ploys can evolve much further away from the ball, as you adapt to a more detailed approach. When team tactics expand to an 8 vs. 8 grouping, the results will be more beneficial if the practice is performed on a field that is getting close to the actual regulation-size field. (See Diagram 2-8.)

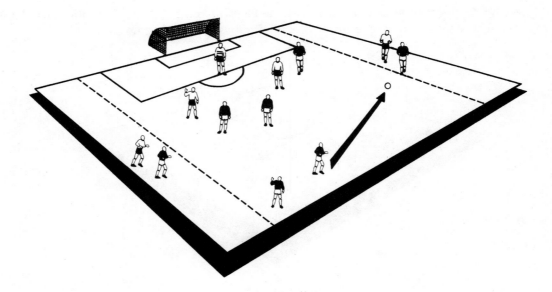

DIAGRAM 2-8
TEAM TACTICS
In a 7 vs. 5 situation on a half-field, the offense must move the ball forward in an attempt to score. An attacker and a defender are the only two players allowed in the two lanes on either wing. The emphasis is placed on a 1 vs. 1 down the wings.

CHOOSING DRILLS AND PRACTICES

The choice of a certain drill or practice will depend on the two areas already discussed:

- which playing position is chosen
- which coaching level is chosen

Both areas will determine what drill is to be used and when it will be used.

SECTION
THREE

Progressive Soccer
Practice

CHAPTER 3

1st Man Offense
Player With the Ball:
Control

COACHING POINTS

In order to deny the opposition any forward movement, a team must look to regain and retain possession of the ball. If a team is to utilize space, it must first create it through the player's ability, not only in knowing how to control the ball but also in knowing when and where to control it. A player can gain control of the ball after it has been passed from a teammate or it has been intercepted from the opponent. A player must be aware that certain principles of controlling a ball have to be mastered if possession is to be maintained.

Approach

Move Into the Path of the Ball

Anticipating the flight and speed of the ball is necessary to time the movement of the body so that the ball will not be missed. Initially a player should learn how to anticipate and control balls that are played along the ground.

Different parts of the foot can be used for controlling the ball, such as the inside, the outside, the sole, and the instep. The ball can be played directly toward a player in a stationary position and then to either side of him. The more proficient a player becomes with this technique, the wider the ball can be placed. The player should plan his move early to give himself more time to make other decisions. He can move forward in an attempt to be first to the ball and when he has the ball under control, pass it back to the server. It is best if the ball can be controlled and passed back to the server in one movement. However, the player must not rush his pass and form bad passing habits.

Young players will very often need more time to settle the ball before deciding what their next move will be but as they become more proficient in this area, they will need less time to make a decision. One of the biggest disadvantages to stopping a ball completely is that a stationary ball can lead to a stationary player. When this happens, a defense can organize itself much easier than when the player with the ball maintains smooth movement in different directions.

If a ball is played in the air and has to be controlled, the player must still move into the path of the ball. Learning to time this movement can be difficult for a player because now he is confronted with having to move backward or forward as well as right or left.

Decide Which Part of the Body to Use

The decision as to which part of the body is to be used should be made early. If a ball is played along the ground, the decision is not difficult to make—the foot will be the body part selected. Likewise, a ball that is coming toward the chest will be controlled with the chest. A ball that is dropping can be controlled with the thigh, chest, or foot. Many beginners have difficulty making the correct decision early enough—they can often be seen lifting their foot too high to meet a ball that would be better controlled by using the thigh.

Contact

Cushion the Ball

The controlling surface is withdrawn on impact to absorb the pace of the ball. If a ball has to be controlled out of the air, the player should attempt to get the ball down to the feet as quickly as possible in order to perform the next technique. The chest, thigh, and foot are the parts of the body used most frequently in controlling a ball.

Chest

This is the largest area of the body and can be likened to a large pillow or cushion that absorbs whatever hits it. The surface is immediately withdrawn as the ball touches the chest so as to cushion and therefore prevent the ball from rebounding out of control. [See Photo Series 3-1.]

PHOTO SERIES 3-1
CONTROLLING THE BALL WITH THE CHEST

(A)
Approach
Moving into the path of the ball

(B)
Contact
Deciding to use the chest as the controlling surface

**PHOTO SERIES 3-1
CONTROLLING THE BALL WITH THE CHEST
(Cont'd)**

(C)
<u>Follow-through</u>
**Cushioning the ball
down to the feet
to continue the
movement**

Thigh

There is more of a cushioning effect with this part of the body due to the muscle mass in contact with the ball. The actual part of the thigh that is used can be marked at the bottom of the player's shorts. [See Photo Series 3-2.]

**PHOTO SERIES 3-2
CONTROLLING THE BALL WITH THE THIGH**

(A)
<u>Approach</u>
**Moving the thigh
into the path of the
ball**

(B)
<u>Contact</u>
**Cushioning the ball
with the thigh**

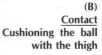

**PHOTO SERIES 3-2
CONTROLLING THE BALL WITH THE THIGH
(Cont'd)**

(C)
Follow-through
The ball is then controlled down to the feet to continue the movement

Foot

Different parts of the foot can be used successfully depending upon what the player's next move will be. [See Photo Series 3-3.]

- Inside—This is the largest area of the foot and the most frequently used. A beginning player will make this surface the only form of control even though it has the major disadvantage of breaking the stride pattern if the player is attempting to control the ball while moving. This is due to the awkward position of the foot, which must be turned outward to receive the ball in balance.

- Outside—Beginning players should be encouraged to use this part of the foot because of its effectiveness in setting up the ball for a drive pass or a shot. The ball can be squeezed to the outside of the player's body with very little effort or foot readjustment. This is done with a smooth movement which can also disguise the player's intentions to a defender. However, some players do have difficulty making the slight adjustment needed to push the ball out to the side and out in front. They will usually overplay one or the other.

- Instep—This is normally used when a ball is dropping and the player has time to control without interference from the opposition. It can also be used when moving in stride to take the pace off the ball without completely bringing the ball to a stop.

- Sole—Use of this part of the foot is often referred to as the wedge trap: the ball is wedged between the sole of the foot and the ground. However, with the ball stopped in this manner, defenders can close in quickly and force the player with the ball to react too quickly in making his next move. Beginning players will use this form of control to line up for the push pass.

PHOTO SERIES 3-3
CONTROLLING THE BALL WITH THE FOOT

(A)
Controlling with the
inside of the foot

(B)
Controlling with the
outside of the foot

(C)
Controlling with the
instep of the foot

(D)
Controlling with the
sole of the foot

Follow-through

Move the Ball

Moving the ball after it has been controlled will take the form of either a shot, pass, or dribble. Players should not keep their eyes on the ball all through its flight. Instead, they should quickly check out their surroundings to see what possibilities will lie ahead once the ball is at their feet. Advanced players will have done this even before the ball is played. This awareness of the possibilities allows for more fluid movement once the player has control because he does not have to be looking up and down. If a player is in a realistic shooting position, then shooting should be his first choice. If not, he should determine what passing possibilities are available to maintain possession. If all players are tightly marked but there is space available to go forward, the player should advance with the ball himself.

A smooth performance can aid immensely in the movements immediately following control. A player who decided to shoot may not have controlled the ball in such a manner that would allow a shot to take place. He must therefore perform an alternate movement.

Controlling a ball is a means to an end. Players must be aware of what options are open to them in order to be productive in the different areas of the field. It is important to teach beginners "ball awareness" early in their development. Knowledge of what the ball will do after it has made contact with different parts of the body will help the player master fundamental techniques. For example, a ball that is spinning excessively when received is much more difficult to control than one that is not spinning. Players who are shown this spin early in their training will react and perform much more productively in their later development.

Juggling the ball can offer practice in this area. Teach the players to experiment with the ball in a manner that will allow them to discover for themselves that a spinning ball can be mastered. [See Photo Series 3-4.] A spinning ball can often lead to a breakdown in performance simply because players do not know how to adjust a technique to compensate for this spin. A good example of this can be seen when the ball is played across the penalty area

PHOTO SERIES 3-4
JUGGLING THE BALL WITH DIFFERENT
PARTS OF THE BODY

(A)
Juggling with the thigh

(B)
Juggling with the foot

PHOTO SERIES 3-4
JUGGLING THE BALL WITH DIFFERENT PARTS OF THE BODY
(Cont'd)

(C)
Juggling with the
head

from the right-wing to a player who is running toward the goal to take a shot. Many times the ball goes wide to the left of the goal. Players should realize that the majority of balls played in this fashion are spinning toward the left side because they have been propelled from the right side. Players can compensate for the spin of the ball by continued practice with balls that are played in from different directions at different speeds. Players who keep the ball on the ground aid in keeping the game simple. Most balls played in the air result in a lack of team control. When control is lost the ability to play an offensive game is lost.

DRILLS

DRILL #1

PLAYING POSITION: 1ST MAN OFFENSE/CONTROL

COACHING LEVEL: WITHOUT OPPOSITION

KEY COACHING POINTS: APPROACH, CONTACT, & FOLLOW-THROUGH

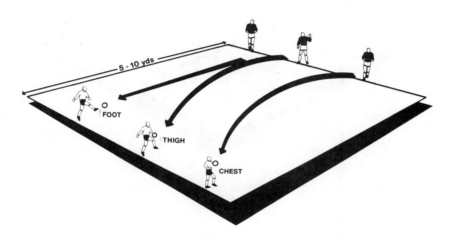

DIAGRAM 3-1

Pair off two players 5–10 yards apart. One player serves the ball to his partner who then controls the ball with the part of the body that you feel needs to be worked on. When using the feet, different parts of the foot can be used. When serving the ball to the chest it is important that the player deliver the ball with very little height. The chest-pass in basketball is an excellent demonstration of the correct service required. Over longer distances this serve will vary. Once a player becomes proficient in dealing with a ball that is served in a straight line, he can move to receive the ball forward, backward, left and right. Each time the player receives the ball, a decision should be made, the body should move, the cushioning should take place, and the follow-through should be performed.

DRILL #2

PLAYING POSITION: 1ST MAN OFFENSE/CONTROL

COACHING LEVEL: PASSIVE OPPOSITION

KEY COACHING POINTS: APPROACH, CONTACT, & FOLLOW-THROUGH

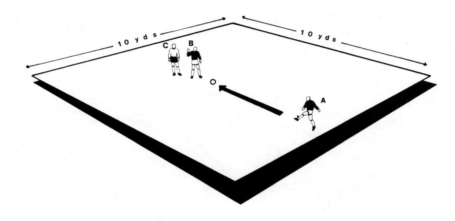

DIAGRAM 3-2

The introduction of a passive defender requires that the player receiving the ball be made more aware of his surroundings. Any defending player around the ball will restrict the time and space of the player who is attempting to control the ball. Player A passes the ball to player B; player C must be close enough to player B to create a defensive problem. At this point player C need not make any attempt to win the ball as his mere presence adds sufficient distraction. The ball can be played to the feet, chest, or thigh.

In all aspects of control the player has had to make decisions surrounding *when* and *where* he must control the ball. There are also decisions dealing with *how* to control the ball. The coach should emphasize:

- Move
- Decide
- Cushion
- Continue

Unless a player can learn the very raw fundamentals involved in controlling a ball, possession will be given up to the opposition, resulting in a total breakdown of offensive soccer.

DRILL#3

PLAYING POSITION: 1ST MAN OFFENSE/CONTROL

COACHING LEVEL: POSITIVE OPPOSITION

KEY COACHING POINTS: WHEN & WHERE TO CONTROL

Controlling the Ball When Facing an Opponent

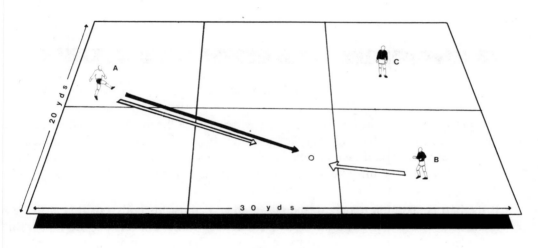

DIAGRAM 3-3

As shown in Diagram 3-3, player A plays the ball into an open space where player B must move and control the ball. Player A follows this pass and attempts to defend against player B. In this 2 vs. 1 situation players C and B must place the ball at the opposite side of the grid on the line.

Another defender can be introduced from behind players B and C to make a recovery run and get goalside of the ball.

- Balls can be served to the feet, chest, and thigh.
- The player controlling the ball must decide if he is to pass or dribble.
- The movements forward should be controlled and done quickly.

Controlling the Ball With the Back to Goal

Diagram 3-4 illustrates a 1 vs. 1 situation in the middle grids. Player A passes the ball to player B who either turns with the ball and passes to player D or passes back to player A. Player C acts as a defender. Players B and C rotate after each service unless there is one particular player who needs work in this area.

- The player receiving the ball should take the player marking him away from the ball and then check back to receive the pass.

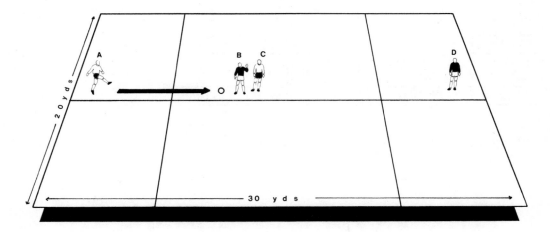

DIAGRAM 3-4

- The player receiving the ball should know which side of the defender is more available to use. Some defenders will overplay one side. If this is not a tactical move then the player receiving should take advantage of this space. A quick glance will very often help in determining this situation, especially if the defender is not marking so close that physical contact will give his whereabouts.

- If the ball is taken on the chest, the player should adjust his body position at the last moment to shield the ball away from the defender while still turning to go past this defender. If the body is adjusted too early, the defender will read his intentions and adapt to the situation.

- If the player is going to control the ball with his foot and turn, he should receive the ball on his outside foot so that the body is screening the ball from the defender. When the ball has been controlled and pushed to the side in one motion, the player can then "spin" and either shoot, pass, or advance the ball. We prefer the term "spin" as opposed to "turn" because of the time factor involved. Players who "turn" normally touch the ball too many times before their next action follows. By spinning around, a more fluid movement results, with a smoother and quicker outcome. If the ball is taken on the outside of the left foot, the player will spin on the sole of his right foot and move around to the left side. This will allow the player to keep in stride.

In an area 30 yards x 20 yards the ball is served from player A to player B. (See Diagram 3-5.) Player C leaves the corner of the last grid and moves to challenge player B. The first touch (control) by player B must be in the last grid after he has moved to meet the ball. Player B must now consider his options. If he has time to turn, player A should inform him. Player B will then have a 1 vs. 1 situation with the intention of scoring a point by placing the ball between two cones spaced 8 yards apart. A goalkeeper can be introduced. If player C closes down player B from behind, B then has the option of playing the ball back to player A for a 2 vs. 1 setting. Other players can be introduced.

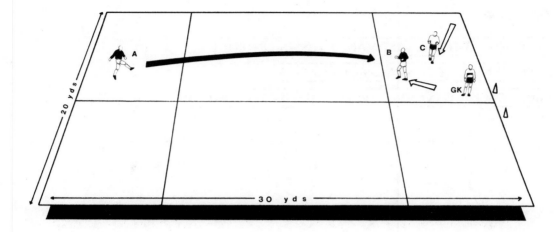

DIAGRAM 3-5

Player B must consider whether to:

• Control the ball and turn.

• Control the ball and shield.

• Control the ball and pass it back to player A.

• Play the ball back first time to player A. This first-time ball can be classified as a form of control even though it is not, in its purest form, collecting and passing.

DRILL #4

PLAYING POSITION: 1ST MAN OFFENSE/CONTROL

COACHING LEVEL: SMALL-SIDED GAME

KEY COACHING POINTS: WHEN & WHERE TO CONTROL

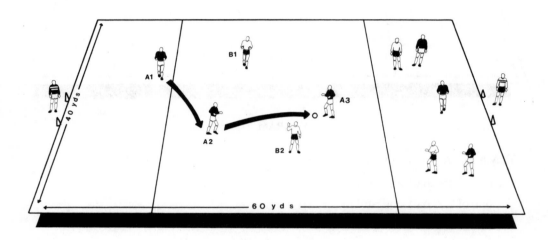

DIAGRAM 3-6

With two groups of six players each, including a goalkeeper, place this condition on the game—the ball is to be in play in the following order:

- Throw
- Control (to the ground)
- Pick up and throw

In this example player A-1 has the ball in his hands. He throws the ball to player A-2 who must control it using different parts of his body. Player A-2 immediately controls the ball down to his feet. Player A-2 then picks up the ball in his hands and throws it to a teammate, player A-3. Player A-3 cannot run with the ball. The opposition must attempt to intercept the ball by placing their bodies in the path of the ball and controlling it or by simply picking up a poorly controlled ball. A goal can be scored from anywhere by a player controlling the ball and then shooting. This exercise is very popular because it generates excitement among players. They can go against tradition within the laws of the game and use their hands. More proficient players can pass the ball to a teammate after it has been controlled from a throw.

- A conditioned game such as this allows a skill to be repeated over and over.
- Intelligent movement off the ball is essential to create space.

DRILL #5

PLAYING POSITION: 1ST MAN OFFENSE/CONTROL

COACHING LEVEL: TEAM TACTICS

KEY COACHING POINTS: WHEN & WHERE TO CONTROL

The purpose at this stage is to achieve quality control in a realistic game situation. This need not be an 11 vs. 11 game. It can take the form of a 7 vs. 5, 8 vs. 8, eventually building up to a full-sided game. The purpose of dealing with a phase of the game is to isolate the skill of control. A player must know not only *how, when,* and *where to control* the ball, but also *how to build up a total team understanding* of what is happening in relation to the time and space allowed by the opposition.

Players who possess the ability to control the ball in tight situations with very little time or space are the foundation on which great teams are built. Performing in team situations is the ultimate goal for which individuals must strive. Teaching control in team situations will allow:

- Players to understand each other
- Players to perform in the most realistic game situation

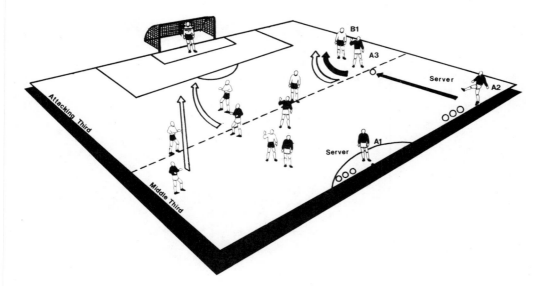

DIAGRAM 3-7

There is now a 7 vs. 5 situation in the middle third and attacking third of the field. Two servers, A-1 and A-2, are positioned on the halfway line. They each have a supply of soccer balls. Offensive players in the attacking third of the field must attempt to get free of their defenders who have been instructed to play strict man-to-man defense. In this example, player A-2 is passing the ball to player A-3 while player B-1 acts as the defender who is assigned to mark the player A-3. As soon as an offensive player has lost his defender and is coming back toward the server, the server will play different balls in to him. Some balls will be to the chest and some will be to the feet. Player A-3 must make a decision based on the locations of the defenders and his teammates. If he has time to control the ball and turn, he should attempt to do so. He can then cross the ball over to his teammates. The control will be performed in tight situations. Defenders will be marking close even if they are playing a zone defense. The closer the ball advances toward the goal, the closer and tighter the defenders will mark.

If you are working on controlling the ball with a player's back to the goal, focus totally on this function. Only repetition of a situation will give players the practice they need. When you are satisfied that this has been achieved, players can then decide whether to:

- Turn with the ball
- Play the ball to another teammate after controlling it without turning
- Play a first-time ball to a teammate
- Shield the ball until help arrives

CHAPTER 4

1st Man Offense
Player With the Ball:
Passing

COACHING POINTS

Playing the ball from one player to another in the form of a pass is the basic means of communication between players on a team. A team that has possession of the ball will use the passing skill more than any other to maintain possession. Good habits must be established from the very beginning. To establish these, three points must be acknowledged:

- You yourself, as coach, must instill a disciplined attitude into the player.
- A player must have a range of sound passing techniques.
- The player must perform the correct technique at the correct time.

Of all the skills that are used in the game of soccer, passing is the one you should pay the most attention to in the framework of progression. If players are struggling to pass a ball without the presence of any opposition, then there are no grounds on which to introduce any form of distraction. Players who cannot pass over short distances on the ground should not begin to work on passing long balls in the air.

In coaching the skill of passing, attention must first be directed toward playing the ball on the ground over a short distance. In each of the following passes, three main areas will be dealt with:

- Approach
- Contact
- Follow-through

Each of these areas is common to all passes. If you observe a breakdown in a player's passing technique, it is important to determine whether this breakdown is due to the player's approach, contact, or follow-through, or whether it is a combination of these.

Push Pass

This is the most accurate of all the passes due to its reliability over short distances. Technique for the push pass is illustrated in Diagrams 4-1 through 4-3 and in Photo Series 4-1.

Approach

In moving forward to make contact with the ball, the angle a player takes is a straight line toward his intended target. This, as will be seen later, is different from the approach for a drive pass which requires a much wider angle.

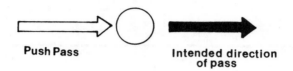

Push Pass   **Intended direction of pass**

DIAGRAM 4-1
ANGLE OF APPROACH FOR THE PUSH PASS

One of the biggest problems youngsters have in attempting to learn the push pass is in the approach. They have a tendency to approach the ball from the side, while still trying to make contact with the inside of the foot. It is a very awkward movement because it usually causes the player to stop before swinging a mechanical leg into the ball, with practically no flow or rhythm to the action. Players will sometimes respond better if they can first walk into the ball, a slow-motion approach that allows players to see their steps up close. A stationary ball is a valuable training aid for these early stages.

For a proper approach, the nonkicking foot should be placed at the side of the ball, pointing in the intended direction of the pass. The distance of this foot from the ball should allow for free-swinging movement of the kicking leg.

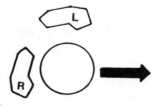

DIAGRAM 4-2
FOOT PLACEMENT PRIOR TO CONTACT

Contact

The inside of the foot makes contact with the midsection of the ball. The foot is turned outward and the ankle locked firm.

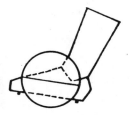

DIAGRAM 4-3
CONTACT AREA FOR THE PUSH PASS

The head should be over the ball with the eyes looking down at it. The contact on the ball is the most important area to stress.

Follow-Through

Once contact has been made and the ball has started its movement toward a teammate, accuracy can be maintained if the follow-through of the kicking leg is aimed in the same direction as the intended target. A correct follow-through will prevent the habit of allowing the kicking leg to come across the body.

A ball will often travel in the same direction that the kicking leg is pointing. Players should be taught to exaggerate their follow-through as much as possible, especially in the early stages of learning this technique. If a player has difficulty extending this leg, encourage the player to take an extra step in the same direction as the ball. This will also prevent the follow-through from being stopped immediately after contact has been made.

PHOTO SERIES 4-1
THE PUSH PASS

(A)
Approach
Approaching the ball for a push pass

(B)
Approach
Foot placement alongside the ball

PHOTO SERIES 4-1
THE PUSH PASS
(Cont'd)

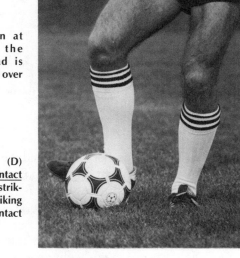

(C)
Contact
Body position at contact on the ball—the head is held steady and over the ball

(D)
Contact
Positions of the striking and nonstriking feet at contact

(E)
Follow-through
Position of the kicking leg on follow-through

Along with the greater accuracy achieved through the push pass and the ease with which it controls the ball, possession of the ball can also be maintained. There are however, two disadvantages to the push pass. First, it is not a very powerful pass and second, it can be a very predictable pass. Even so, the strengths outweigh the weaknesses.

Drive Pass

The drive pass is used to play the ball over a greater distance than the push pass. There are many similarities between the drive pass and the technique of shooting.

The drive pass can be a difficult technique for young players to learn because of the required locking of the ankle with the toes pointing down. They find it hard to move the small area of the laces through the midsection of the ball. Technique for the drive pass is illustrated in Diagrams 4-4 and 4-5 and in Photo Series 4-2.

Approach

The player will now move toward the ball from a slight angle of about 30 degrees. The main reason for this type of approach is to give the kicking leg a larger sweep in which to acquire power. If a strong pass is intended, the last stride before making contact is usually longer than the previous strides. This provides more distance through which the leg can drive before contact is made.

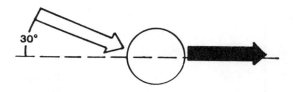

DIAGRAM 4-4
ANGLE OF APPROACH FOR THE DRIVE PASS

The nonkicking foot should be positioned alongside the ball so that a full leg swing can be accomplished. If a pass is intended to be played in the air, the nonkicking foot will be slightly behind the ball.

Contact

The ankle should be locked firm with the toes pointing down toward the ground. This will allow the instep (laces) to make contact with the midsection of the ball. If the player fails to lock the ankle, his toes will begin to lift up and the contact will be made with the toes. Young players often attempt to kick with their toes because this action requires little rearranging of the foot position as they run forward.

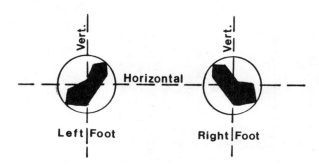

DIAGRAM 4-5
POSITION OF THE FOOT AT CONTACT

A player must make contact below the midsection of the ball if he intends to drive the ball into the air. Going above other players' heads can be an effective method of clearing the ball from the defense.

Follow-through

The kicking leg should be extended forward in the same line as the intended direction of the ball. There should be very little follow-through action across the body because this would force the hips out of alignment with the ball's intended line of travel. Instead of the hips' being square to the pass, they would begin to roll in toward the nonkicking foot, thus preventing the ball from traveling in the most direct path.

PHOTO SERIES 4-2
THE DRIVE PASS

(A)
Approach
Moving into the ball for the drive pass

(B)
Contact
Position of the foot and knee at contact

(C)
Follow-through
Body position exaggerating the follow-through

Swerve Pass—Inside

The swerve pass that is made with the inside of the foot can be deceiving to defenders and very hard for them to judge when they attempt to intercept the ball. Many players will use this swerve as a shooting technique. It is also effective at set plays, such as a direct free-kick or from a corner kick. Technique for the inside swerve pass is illustrated in Diagram 4-6 and in Photo Series 4-3.

Approach

The approach is very similar to the drive pass, with the nonkicking foot again being placed next to the ball, but now slightly behind it. This foot is still directed forward, but it has little effect on where the ball will travel, as now the direction is determined by the amount of spin and power applied on the ball.

Contact

The ball is struck by the inside of the foot after the kicking foot has come across the ball from left to right. (This is for a right-footed pass.) The area of contact is slightly right of the center of the ball. This allows the ball to rotate right to left with the swerve also being from right to left—inside swerve.

DIAGRAM 4-6
AREA OF CONTACT FOR THE INSIDE SWERVE PASS

If the pass is to travel through the air the contact must be made just below the midsection. Sound contact is a necessity to impart any productive spin.

Follow-through

One of the few exceptions to the rule that the kicking leg moves in the same direction as the intended pass can be found in the swerve pass. The follow-through of this leg will move away from the body after contact has been made.

PHOTO SERIES 4-3
THE INSIDE SWERVE PASS

(A)
<u>Contact</u>
Placement of the foot on the ball

(B)
<u>Follow-through</u>
Outward movement of the kicking leg providing the swerve

(C)
<u>Follow-through</u>
Continued movement of the kicking leg away from the body

Swerve Pass—Outside

This pass is similar to the one made with the inside of the foot. The main difference is that the spin is now placed on the opposite side of the ball and with a different part of the foot. It is an effective means to disguise the intentions of the player passing the ball. Technique for the outside swerve pass is illustrated in Diagram 4-7 and in Photo Series 4-4.

Approach

The movement into the ball will be from a straight-on position. This will allow for the kicking leg to come across the body in a slashing action. The nonkicking foot will be placed slightly behind the ball and directed in the same line as the approach.

Contact

The ball is struck with the outside of the foot after this kicking foot has come across the ball from right to left. (This is for a right-footed pass.) The area of contact is slightly to the left of the center of the ball. This allows the ball to rotate left to right with the swerve also being from left to right—outside swerve.

DIAGRAM 4-7
AREA OF CONTACT FOR THE OUTSIDE SWERVE PASS

Follow-through

The kicking leg will follow through across the body to enhance the slashing action. Again, this is an exception to the rule that the kicking leg moves in the direction of the intended pass.

PHOTO SERIES 4-4
THE OUTSIDE SWERVE PASS

(A)
Contact
Placement of the foot on the ball

(B)
Follow-through
Position of the kicking leg across the body after contact has been made

Chip Pass

The chip pass can be used to get the ball behind defenders and to players who are in tight spaces. This can be effective when a player needs to play the ball over a defender's head to a teammate who is marked by another defender. Contact technique for the chip pass is illustrated in Photo 4-5.

Approach

The player will move into the ball from a slight angle. The nonkicking foot is placed closer to the ball than the normal position found in many of the other passes, 4-5 inches.

Contact

The knee of the kicking leg should be flexed as high as possible before being straightened as it moves down toward the ball. The area of the instep closest to the toes will come into contact with the ball at a point where it touches the ground. This action imparts backspin on the ball as it rises quickly.

Follow-through

There is very little follow-through as the kicking foot stops immediately after contact has been made. For longer chip passes the knee can be raised quickly up to the chest area after contact has been made.

PHOTO 4-5
THE CHIP PASS

Contact
Low position of the
foot when striking
the ball

Volley Pass—Instep

This pass is used when there is an urgency to get the ball away quickly. It can be used over long distances where the ball must be cleared out of the defense or it can be used as a shot on goal. Because of the timing involved in playing a ball in the air, this can be a difficult skill for some players to acquire. Approach technique for the instep volley pass is illustrated in Photo 4-6.

Approach

The player moves straight in to meet the ball. The arms are placed out from the side to balance the body. The head should be placed over the ball. The nonkicking foot points toward the target and is placed behind the ball. The kicking leg is lifted up so that the kicking foot is level with the ball.

Contact

The ankle is extended with the toes pointing down toward the ground. Contact on the ball is made with the instep to the midsection. Every attempt should be made to prevent the ball from rising quickly. If the pass is intended to travel over a long distance, the player must judge where on the ball he must strike to give the correct elevation.

Follow-through

The kicking leg will move toward the intended target staying above the ball for as long as possible if a low pass is required.

PHOTO 4-6
THE INSTEP VOLLEY PASS

Approach
Body position prior
to contact

Volley Pass—Inside

This pass is used over short distances when a player has insufficient time in which to control the ball first. Contact technique for the inside volley pass is illustrated in Photo 4-7.

Approach

The player will move in to the ball from a slight angle. This angle will allow the foot to be turned outward. The nonkicking foot is positioned slightly behind the ball with the head over the ball and the arms out for balance.

Contact

The ankle is locked in the same position as for the push pass. The inside of the foot is the contact area used. The ball should be struck at the midsection to allow greater accuracy over a short distance.

Follow-through

There is not as much follow-through with the inside volley pass as there is with the instep volley. The inside of the foot is used to change the direction of the ball with little forward movement after contact has been made.

PHOTO 4-7
THE INSIDE VOLLEY PASS

Contact
Kicking leg is raised for the correct position of the kicking foot

Developing Passing Game Skills

Players must be aware of their surroundings on a soccer field. All the prior techniques cannot be performed unless a player is familiar with his role in a skill situation. Teammates and opposition are both a help and a hindrance in all situations. How a player deals with this is a reflection of how well he understands these situations. It is therefore important for a player to be aware of:

- Where teammates are
- Where the opposition is

One of the major faults to be found in young players is their inability to lift their heads and look around. Teammates and opponents can be located only if the player with the ball surveys his surroundings.

A player who is proficient in the techniques of different passes must also be able to apply them in the skill setting. This becomes more complex because of the presence of teammates and opponents. Besides the fundamental techniques required for the various passes, there are four additional skills that are the criteria for success in moving the ball from one player to another in the game situation. These are:

- Accuracy
- Power
- Timing
- Disguise

All of these are related in some form or another.

Accuracy

This is the ability to move the ball over a certain distance with any chosen part of the foot or head, so that it reaches its target and possession is maintained. Accuracy is the first priority for players who are learning the skill of passing.

Power

This is sometimes referred to as the pace of the pass; it is the speed at which the ball travels. Young players usually have difficulty in this area due to the physical limitations of their young bodies. If the pass is too soft it will be intercepted or it will fail to reach the target. If it is too strong it will go out of bounds or beyond the receiving player, making it difficult to control and risking loss of possession. A player should assess the angles and distances, hence the need to practice not only with the ball but with cooperating and opposing players.

Timing

This concerns the release of the ball. The correct moment to release a pass is when it places the opponent in the position of greatest disadvantage. To do this, a player must have the ability to assess and evaluate the relative positions of players around the ball. This ability stems from the confidence and willingness of the player with the ball to look away from it. The essence of good timing is not in the player's ability to keep his eye on the ball, but rather in his ability to look around, assess the possibilities, and release the ball accordingly.

Disguise

Without the ability to disguise a pass it becomes difficult for the player with the ball to cause problems for the opposition—everything becomes predictable. Disguise may be aided by use of the body in feinting or through the eyes and voice in a distracting manner.

In all passing situations players must be aware of:

- Who is available to receive a pass
- The space created for a player to receive the pass

Quality passing involves the four major skill principles previously mentioned for the player with the ball. Cooperating players also assist a situation by their movements off the ball. Players can produce effective combination play by the positional advantage they create for each other.

The development of offensive soccer is dependent upon the correct movements of players who are prepared and willing to move.

When to Play to Feet and When to Play to Space

This has been an issue of discussion among coaches for many years. Different styles of play from different countries lead to many different approaches. An open style of soccer, which includes the "long ball" played into space, will result in a different approach to coaching than the "tight ball" possession played elsewhere.

It is important to stress that at the early stages of learning the game, players should be encouraged to pass the ball to feet most of the time. This does not necessarily imply that players will always pass the ball straight at each other. *The ball should be passed so that the player receiving it, wherever he is on the field, is in an area most advantageous to him. He should receive the ball at his feet at the exact moment he wants it.*

There are many through-balls wasted because they are played into open space without any thought given to the area that the receiving player can best utilize. In the defensive and middle thirds of the field possession is the key factor and therefore playing to feet is the required task. In the attacking third of the field players must be prepared to take risks and along with the risks comes the chance of an intercepted pass. They must still attempt the difficult through-ball in order to move the ball alongside and behind the defense. Without forward movement the game of soccer would be merely a scientific exercise.

Movement away from the ball in the form of different kinds of runs will be discussed under the 3rd Man Offense.

The following drills can be modified to incorporate the different kinds of passes that are being taught.

DRILLS

DRILL #1

| PLAYING POSITION: 1ST MAN OFFENSE/PASSING |

| COACHING LEVEL: WITHOUT OPPOSITION |

| KEY COACHING POINTS: APPROACH, CONTACT, & FOLLOW-THROUGH |

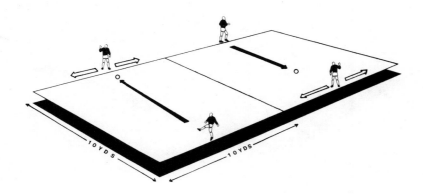

DIAGRAM 4-8

The drill illustrated in Diagram 4-8 gives players practice in passing in pairs, in a 10-yard x 10-yard grid. The players face each other on either side of the grid. The ball is passed in a straight line on the ground with the inside of the foot. The ball should be controlled before it is passed. A realistic goal, such as ten successful passes, should be set for the players to achieve. First-time balls can also be played. Players can be encouraged to move sideways after their partners have controlled the ball. This will encourage players to lift their heads in order to see where to pass the ball. Accuracy must be stressed at all times.

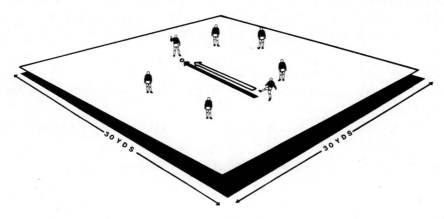

DIAGRAM 4-9

A group of players forms a circle, as shown in Diagram 4-9. The drill begins with one ball being played across the circle. As soon as the player has released the pass he follows it across to the player receiving it. After this pass has been controlled it is again played across the circle and immediately followed. Players should call out the name of the player for whom the ball is intended. Additional balls can be introduced at the appropriate time. When more balls are introduced confusion can arise if players do not assess a situation before reacting to it. In this way, players learn to think ahead of the ball. Overloading the drill with too many balls is counterproductive, as it places the players in a totally unrealistic drill.

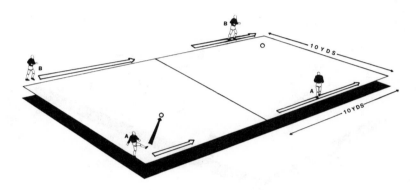

DIAGRAM 4-10

Offensive players who remain stationary throughout a game present very few problems for a defense. A defense will have to reorganize quickly, however, when players away from the ball begin to move. Not only should a player know how to pass a ball to a teammate who is stationary but, more important, he should be capable of finding players who are working to become open for a pass.

An excellent means to familiarize players with this aspect of the game is through grid work. Two players are positioned in the corners of a 10-yard x 10-yard grid directly opposite each other. (See Diagram 4-10.) Player A passes the ball diagonally across the grid to the corner. Player B runs down his side of the grid toward the same corner. The ball should arrive at the same time that player B arrives. After player A has released the ball he begins to run down his own side to the corner. The drill will then begin again moving back to the initial corners.

It is important to stress that:

• Even though accuracy has been attained, the players must still concentrate on the target area.

• The ball should be paced firmly so as to arrive in the corner at the same time as the teammate does.

• The ball should be released at the correct time so as to arrive at the same time as the teammate.

You can vary the drill by asking the player without the ball to begin his run, check back, and then continue his run. This change of direction and pace will force the player with the ball to look up before making the pass.

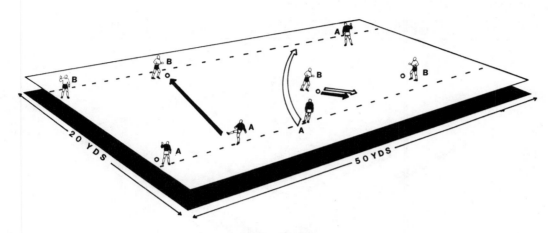

DIAGRAM 4-11

Not only should a player be capable of passing the ball to a player who is already in a forward position, but he should also understand what is required in playing a ball forward to a player making a run from behind. In an area of 20 yards x 50 yards, players A and B are positioned 15–20 yards apart. (See Diagram 4-11.) Player A passes the ball ahead of player B. Player A then begins to make an overlapping run behind player B. As this is occurring, player B is moving the ball in one controlling movement, across his body before turning and giving a similar ball back to player A.

This drill is further developed in the 3rd Man Offense section. It is used at this stage of a player's development to give him the feeling of:

- Passing to a player who is moving
- Passing the ball while he himself is moving
- Moving after passing the ball

DRILL #2

PLAYING POSITION: 1ST MAN OFFENSE/PASSING

COACHING LEVEL: PASSIVE OPPOSITION

KEY COACHING POINTS: APPROACH, CONTACT, & FOLLOW-THROUGH

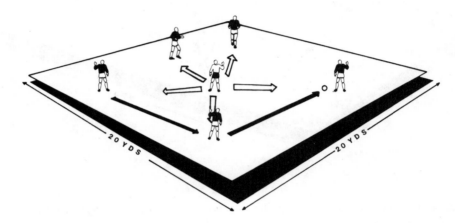

DIAGRAM 4-12

In an area 20 yards x 20 yards five offensive players keep possession of the ball. A defender is positioned in the area and conditioned to quickly close down the player with the ball. This defender cannot win the ball by tackling. He can only attempt to intercept the ball once it has been played by the offense. Stress to the defender that his function is to move to the ball quickly to place this player under a limited amount of pressure.

The player in possession must think quickly in order to make a successful pass. Other offensive players can move into positions that will assist this player.

This can be a tiresome drill for the defender, therefore this defender should be rotated frequently. The more proficient the players become in moving the ball around, the fewer offensive players are involved.

- Make sure that the player who is intercepted is not always the player who becomes the defender.

DRILL #3

PLAYING POSITION: 1ST MAN OFFENSE/PASSING

COACHING LEVEL: POSITIVE OPPOSITION

KEY COACHING POINTS: WHEN & WHERE TO PASS

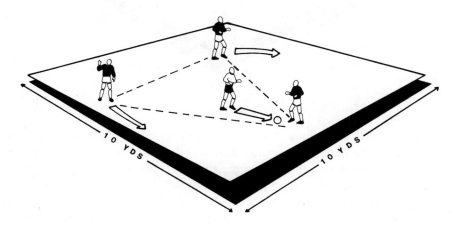

DIAGRAM 4-13

As shown in Diagram 4-13, a 3 vs. 1 situation is staged in a 10-yard x 10-yard area. The defending player becomes active and attempts to win the ball. The player with the ball must now react quickly to the situation. The other two offensive players must move to create two passing possibilities at all times. If the offensive players are continually having difficulty, the grid area can be enlarged. All offensive players should utilize the space that is available in their area by positioning themselves:

- On the grid lines
- At an angle which will prevent the ball from being intercepted

Players not in possession should:

- Think ahead to their next move
- Be aware of moving to a more suitable angle should they not receive the pass
- Know if they should control the ball before passing it
- Communicate with each other

You can freeze the drill and ask the player with the ball to point both hands at the players open for the pass. These imaginary lines should avoid the defender. A triangle is formed with the offensive players positioned at the three corners. Sound effective support is necessary for this drill to be effective.

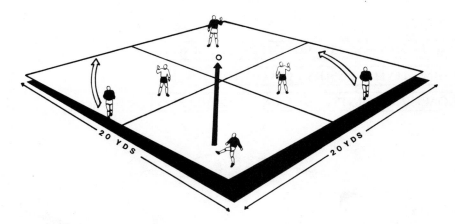

DIAGRAM 4-14

In a 20-yard x 20-yard area a 4 vs. 2 situation is set up. (See Diagram 4-14.) The offensive players must be patient in passing the ball among themselves. The objective is to pass the ball between the two defenders in order to score a point. This is commonly referred to as "splitting the defense." Forcing the ball will only lead to the possibility that the pass will be intercepted. Strong movement off the ball, through positioning at the correct angle, will allow an opportunity for players to utilize the space in between and behind the defenders.

The defenders will allow the easy ball to be played through them if they become "flat." This is a term used when defenders become positioned alongside each other with little or no depth evident. As this is not a defensive drill you need not stress the defensive aspects. Rather, stress:

- The patience needed to perform the drill effectively
- The movement of the players off-the-ball
- The quality pass from the player with the ball
- Communication between players

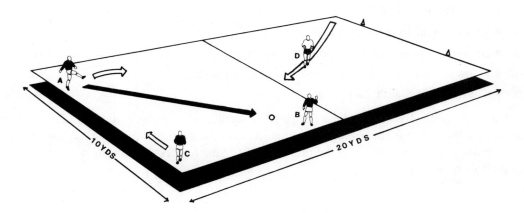

DIAGRAM 4-15

In an area 20 yards x 10 yards three offensive players are positioned in three corners of one grid. (See Diagram 4-15.) A defender is positioned in the corner of the far grid. Two cones are placed 8 yards apart on the end grid line. In this 3 vs. 1 situation, player A passes the ball to player B. As soon as player A has released the ball the defending player D leaves the corner in an attempt to win the ball. Player C offers support for both players. When player B moves for the ball he can:

- Turn with the ball and confront the defender
- Play the ball back immediately to either player A or C
- Shield the ball and then pass it

This 3 vs. 1 situation has developed with direction as the offensive players attempt to place the ball on the end grid line between the cones. An extra defender can be added when progress is evident. The offside law can be applied when the players become proficient in the movements required. The players off the ball should:

- Move into a position to receive the ball
- Support the player with the ball
- Communicate with each other

DRILL #4

| PLAYING POSITION: 1ST MAN OFFENSE/PASSING |
| KEY COACHING POINTS: WHEN & WHERE TO PASS |

PLAYING POSITION: 1ST MAN OFFENSE/PASSING

COACHING LEVEL: SMALL-SIDED GAME

KEY COACHING POINTS: WHEN & WHERE TO PASS

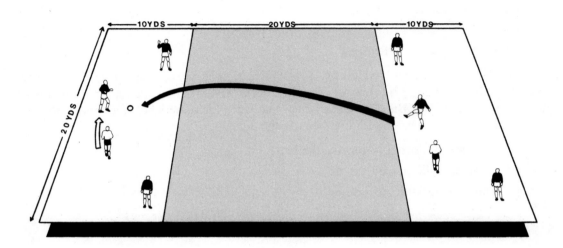

DIAGRAM 4-16

Three offensive players are placed in each of the two defined areas, 20 yards x 10 yards, as illustrated in Diagram 4-16. A defender is placed in each area. A neutral 20-yard area divides both groups. One ball is placed with one group, setting up a 3 vs. 1. As soon as an opportunity emerges when this team can pass the ball through the neutral area to the other three offensive players, this should be encouraged. The defenders should work hard to take the ball away from the offense.

Stress that only certain passes can be used across the neutral area—the push pass, drive pass, chip pass. A restriction can be placed on the number of touches a team is allowed before they must pass the ball across to the other team.

In the same area as for the previous drill, four offensive players are now placed in each of the two outside areas. (See Diagram 4-17.) Two defenders are placed in the area with the team in possession—4 vs. 2. The team in possession must look across the neutral area to the other players who are waiting for a pass. As soon as the ball is played across to this waiting team, the defenders give chase to create another 4 vs. 2 situation. If the defenders can intercept the pass before it reaches the other area they then become offensive players, while two other players become defenders.

The offensive players must show:

• Patience

• Quality passing

• The ability to know when to pass the ball across the neutral area

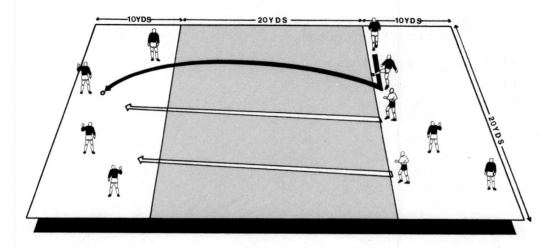

DIAGRAM 4-17

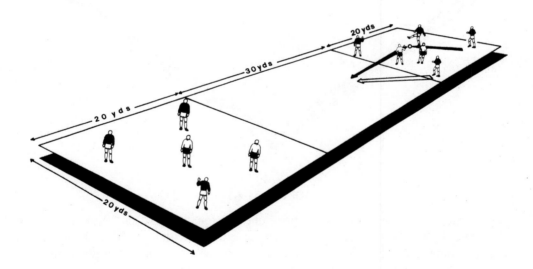

DIAGRAM 4-18

• The ability to realize when a first-time pass is more advantageous than controlling the ball first

Four offensive players are positioned against two defenders in an area 20 yards x 20 yards, as shown in Diagram 4-18. An area of 30 yards x 20 yards separates this first group from a second group of three offensive players against two defenders. The four players in possession of the ball must play it around until a player can pass into the path of a teammate who has moved forward out of his area. This player then runs with the ball into the other area, again creating a 4 vs. 2. Possession is maintained by this team until a similar pass can be made back to the original group.

Both short and long passes can be used, as can the chip pass. Players must time their runs out from the group. The offensive players must:

- Communicate with each other
- Be decisive when they make their run
- Ensure a quality pass

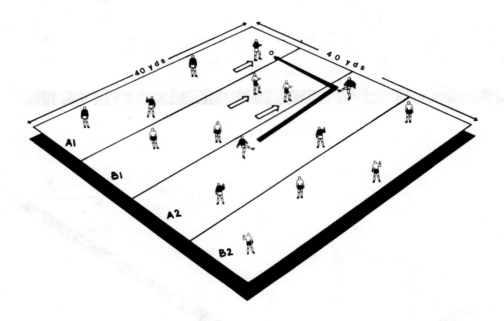

DIAGRAM 4-19

Four teams of equal numbers are positioned in four lanes, each 10 yards x 40 yards. (See Diagram 4-19.) Team A1 is positioned in the end lane with team B1 in the next lane; A2 is positioned next and B2 in the final lane. The ball can be given to any team. In Diagram 4-19 team A2 has possession. They move the ball around in their lane until an opening appears through which they can play the ball to team A1. The defending team, B1, must move to block the through-ball. If A1 has possession they then move the ball around before passing it back to A2 again. If B1 intercepts the ball they will attempt to play the ball to team B2. A certain number of continuous passes can be required before a team wins. Emphasis is placed on:

- Players looking to split two defenders
- Patience in passing the ball
- Players not forcing the ball
- Quality passing throughout
- Players moving to receive a pass

A time limit can be imposed on the drill and on the number of touches by one team.

DRILL #5

PLAYING POSITION: 1ST MAN OFFENSE/PASSING

COACHING LEVEL: TEAM TACTICS

KEY COACHING POINTS: WHEN & WHERE TO PASS COMMUNICATION

Within the Team Tactics level of coaching, various types of passes have to be performed. Players must select one pass over another in different situations. To accelerate the learning process at this level, conditions can be imposed on the game. Those most widely used in the passing phase of a game are:

- Two-touches only for each player.
- One-touch only for each player.
- Balls must be played on the ground.
- Balls must be played directly to feet.
- Balls must be played in the air.
- Balls must be played with certain parts of the foot.
- Defenders must play strict man-to-man defense.
- Short passes must be made.
- Long passes must be made.

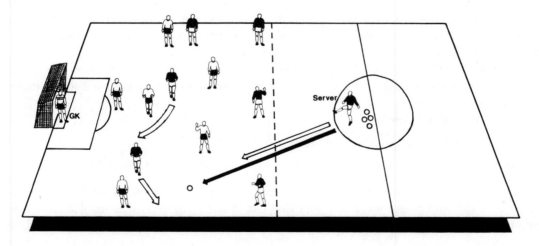

DIAGRAM 4-20

In the attacking third of the field a ball is served in by a player who is also in a supporting role for the offense and a target for the defense. (See Diagram 4-20.) When the attacking team has possession they must move the ball against the defense in an attempt to take a shot on goal. If the defense wins the ball they must play it to the target player in the center circle. Conditions can be imposed.

Players should be encouraged to take risks in the attacking third of the field in order to produce shooting opportunities. This does not necessarily mean that players continually force the ball through the defense. They must be patient, but they must also be quick to take advantage of a situation favorable to the offense.

The offense must concentrate on:

- Splitting the defense with a through-pass
- Getting players alongside and behind the defense
- Taking an early shot

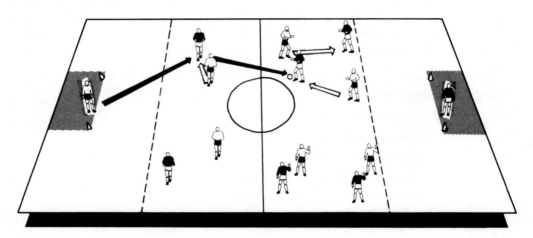

DIAGRAM 4-21

Possession in the middle third of the field is commonly referred to as the "build-up phase." In Diagram 4-21, two teams of 7 vs. 7 are positioned in this area. One player is positioned behind two cones at each end of the midfield area. This player acts as a target for his team as well as a server to the opposition. The team in possession moves the ball around until they can pass through to their target player. Conditions can be imposed for a limited time period.

The offense will work at:

- A patient build-up with short passes
- A long ball to switch the line of approach from one side of the field to the other.

In the defensive third of the field possession cannot be given up to the opposition because of the immediate threat on goal that can result. Any pass that involves a certain amount of risk should not be attempted. The goalkeeper rolls the ball out to a defensive player who plays the ball to another teammate with the intention of locating a target player in the center circle. (See Diagram 4-22.) An alternate drill can begin with this target player passing a ball into the heart of the defense. The defenders would now have to win the ball before bringing it out.

The defense will work at:

- Bringing the ball out down the wings
- Resisting any temptation to dribble
- Playing on the side of safety

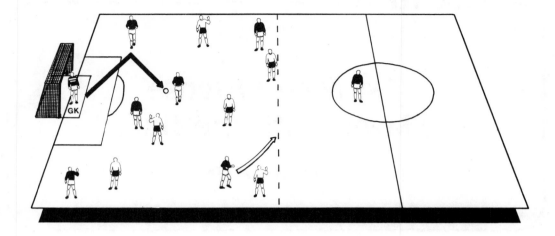

DIAGRAM 4-22

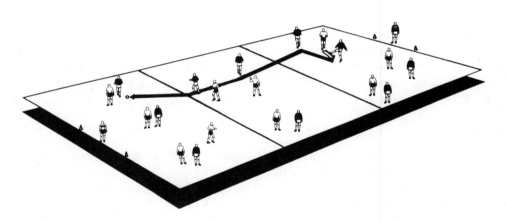

DIAGRAM 4-23

As illustrated in Diagram 4-23, half of a regular soccer field is divided into three equal areas. A goal is placed at each end with a goalkeeper in each. Two teams are divided into defense, midfield, and offense. They are positioned in their respective sections of the field. They cannot move into any other section.

The players work the ball from one section to the other by passing intelligently among themselves and then through into the next section. A shot can be taken only in the section directly in front of goal. Passes can be directed along the ground or in the air depending on what pass is being stressed. Decisions have to be made at some point by the players, as to which pass is more appropriate for a certain situation. They need to realize, through evaluating the surroundings:

- When to play the ball long and when to play the ball short
- When the ball should be played to feet and when it should be played into space
- When to play the ball forward and when to play the ball backward
- When to play the ball wide and when to play the ball through the middle

CHAPTER 5

1st Man Offense Player With the Ball: Shooting

COACHING POINTS

To win games you must score goals; to score goals you must be prepared to shoot. Despite the obvious and straightforward truth of this statement, shooting is probably the most overlooked and underestimated skill in soccer. Shooting is the most important area of offensive soccer. Every skill that is performed, every run that is made, is directed toward the finished shot.

Player Attitude

You have a responsibility to teach players how to shoot, where to shoot, and when to shoot, but a player must have the right attitude before he can shoot. Criticism is very often aimed at a player who fails to score. Failing to score is a breakdown in the technical skills. *Failure to take the shot* is a breakdown in the mental process of a player.

Even before you teach the technical aspects of shooting, give priority to the attitude of the player toward shooting. Once this has been covered, you can then direct attention to the mechanics of the shot. Teaching shooting early in a player's development does not take away from the importance of sound control or quality passing—it simply establishes the importance of shooting in the minds of the players. Structuring a player's thought patterns will lead to a structuring of skills. *When a player receives the ball and has successfully controlled it, or if he intends to play a first-time ball, he must first look to see if he can take a shot.*

One of the most creative moves seen in soccer was in the 1970 World Cup Tournament in Mexico. The great Pelé of Brazil had possession of the ball at the halfway line, when he lifted his head and noticed the opposing goalkeeper was out from his goal line. At that moment Pelé made the decision to take a shot, even though he was well out of the usual shooting range. The shot was unsuccessful as the ball went slightly above the crossbar, but the intention could not be faulted regardless of the outcome. This positive attitude toward shooting was the result of many years of hard work and an understanding of the game.

In adopting the correct mental approach a player can be a step ahead of other players around him. By continually striving to improve his attitude a player can benefit his all-around game and not just his shooting.

The actual time that is spent on shooting has to be as realistic to the game situation as possible. Some coaches avoid shooting drills because of the organizational problems that can occur when large numbers of players and balls appear. One way to handle this is to form small groups, with cones or shirts used as goalposts if portable goals are unavailable. Goalkeepers can be rotated around within a group so as to allow all the players the experience of playing in goal.

With more proficient players you can work on the functions of one or more players in shooting situations or develop a phase of the game in the attacking third of the field.

For players who are learning the skill of shooting, place emphasis first on good contact, using a stationary ball. As soon as progress is evident, introduce a moving ball to capture the realistic shooting opportunities. The ball is rarely stationary when a shot is being taken. It is only at set plays that a player is given the advantage of not having to play a moving ball.

Before taking a shot a player should attempt to:

- Locate where the goalkeeper is positioned
- Decide which area of the goal is more accessible for the shot

Players will sometimes attempt to shoot only when there are no defenders between the ball and the goalkeeper. A good shooting position, however, can be any location on the field from which the goal is within the physical range of the player in possession.

In striking a ball a player must maintain balance throughout and immediately after contact. The player's approach toward the ball can assist immensely with this. A player will have to contend with balls that are moving toward, away from, and across the body. They can be balls on the ground or in the air. What is important is how quickly the player can adjust his body position to react to them.

Shooting—On the Ground

The player who has received the ball to his feet has more chance of being accurate than the player who has to strike it in the air. Once the ball is in a position to be struck, the player must be aware of his approach, contact, and follow-through.

Approach

This will be from the side to allow the kicking leg to generate power by moving through a wider angle. Because of the congested area normally found with shooting positions, however, it is not always possible to approach from an angle.

The nonkicking foot is extremely important in shooting. Many players do not pay enough attention to the placement of this foot. Diagrams 5-1 through 5-3 illustrate approach technique for the nonkicking foot.

For balls that are moving away from the player, the nonkicking foot is placed slightly beyond the ball. This will allow the ball to be alongside the nonkicking foot at the same time the striking foot comes into contact with the ball.

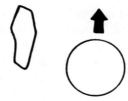

DIAGRAM 5-1
POSITION OF THE NONKICKING FOOT FOR BALLS THAT ARE MOVING AWAY
FROM THE PLAYER

For balls that are moving toward the player, the nonkicking foot is placed slightly behind the ball. This is to allow the ball to be directly alongside the nonkicking foot at the same time the striking foot comes into contact with the ball.

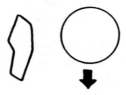

DIAGRAM 5-2
POSITION OF THE NONKICKING FOOT FOR BALLS THAT ARE MOVING
TOWARD THE PLAYER

For balls that are moving across the body, the nonkicking foot should be placed slightly wide of the ball. This will allow the ball to move closer to this foot, while the kicking leg sweeps through to make contact. This is a difficult shot to make because of the timing involved. In all placements of the nonkicking foot the direction is always toward the goal.

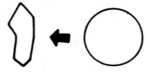

DIAGRAM 5-3
POSITION OF THE NONKICKING FOOT FOR BALLS THAT ARE MOVING ACROSS
THE PLAYER

Contact

The contact area is located on the instep (laces), although some shots can be made with the inside or outside of the foot. It is important for players to place greater emphasis on accuracy than on power. The kicking foot should be firmly locked with the toes pointing toward the ground. The center of the ball should be struck to assist in the intended direction of the shot. Any contact below this point will result in the ball's rising above the goal. It is a much greater mistake to hit a ball over the goal than to place it wide. Any ball that is going wide has a chance to be deflected, either into the goal or out of bounds for a corner kick.

The head should be held steady and the knee placed directly over the ball to assist in keeping it low. One of the hardest shots for a goalkeeper to stop is a low ball played along the ground. The path that a ball takes on the ground is much harder for a goalkeeper to assess than the path of a ball in the air. A goalkeeper will also have problems with a ball that is played low because of the uneven ground which is usually found in a goal area.

By placing his arms out to the side, a player can maintain a more stable base throughout the shot and achieve better balance. If correct contact is made on the ball there is little chance for error.

Follow-through

After contact has been made, the kicking leg must continue to move in the direction of the goal. If this kicking leg is brought across the body, the ball will have a tendency to be hooked.

Shooting—In the Air

A ball that is bouncing will not change direction drastically while still in the air. The problem with striking such a ball is in the awkward positioning of the body that must accompany the technique. There is very little time in which to think before acting. If time were available, a player would most likely try to control the ball first. The timing of this shot is difficult to master at any level of performance.

Volley Shot

There are two forms of shooting the ball on the volley:

- Straight-on Volley
- Sideways Volley

Straight-on Volley

Approach

This will be from behind the ball with little movement from the side. The nonkicking foot is placed behind the ball as it drops. This will allow enough room for the kicking leg to move smoothly into the ball. The arms should be used to balance the body as now the kicking leg is suspended in the air longer than for a ground shot.

Contact

The kicking foot makes contact with the top half or upper section of the ball if at all possible. Any contact beneath will cause the ball to rise. Some players will allow the ball to drop close to the ground before striking it to improve their chance of keeping the ball low, while deriving more power.

If defenders are in the immediate area of the ball there is an urgency to take the shot early by making contact just below waist height. The nonkicking foot can also be extended up on the toes to place as much of the knee over the ball as possible.

The instep (laces) is used to strike the ball as this area of the foot requires minimum rearranging. The toes are pointed down and the ankle held firm.

Follow-Through

The kicking leg will move toward the goal immediately after contact has been made. The head has to be held steady during this period as the eyes focus in on the ball.

Sideways Volley

This is probably the most difficult shot in soccer, other than the infrequently used overhead bicycle kick. The difficulty with this shot derives from the fact that the body is falling away from the ball. Balancing the body throughout this shot is of the utmost importance. Technique for the sideways volley is illustrated in Photo Series 5-1.

Approach

The body is positioned sideways to the flight of the ball. The shoulder that is closest to the goal should fall away to allow the kicking foot to sweep through the upper half of the ball. The nonkicking foot is placed in a position to point toward the goal. This will allow the hips to open up and give the kicking leg a fuller swing. The body will rotate on the nonkicking leg.

Contact

The kicking foot points away from the body. The ankle is held firm and the instep strikes the ball through the upper half. This ensures that the shot is driven downward.

Follow-Through

After the kicking leg has swung forward it continues across the body and down toward the ground.

PHOTO SERIES 5-1
THE SIDEWAYS VOLLEY

(A)
<u>Approach</u>
Moving into position—notice the position of the nonkicking foot opening up the body

(B)
<u>Contact</u>
Balanced body position at contact

PHOTO SERIES 5-1
THE SIDEWAYS VOLLEY
(Cont'd)

(C)
Follow-through
Bringing the kicking
leg across and down

In shooting with any kind of swerve from the inside or outside part of the foot, the technique is the same as that in passing the ball with swerve on it. One of the most productive situations in which to use the swerve shot is from a dead-ball tactic. Here the player can take time to ensure that the correct contact is made.

A part of the skill of shooting is learning to perform movements in tight situations. A player is not always facing the goal before taking a shot; there are occasions when a player will have to receive a pass with his back to goal. Situations such as these require a player to combine the techniques of turning with the ball and shooting with the ball.

A player who turns with the ball can be at a disadvantage if there are defenders in the immediate area of his turn. It is difficult to position the body in the correct form for every shot, but the player can yield positive results by concentrating on the most important aspect of shooting—making good contact with the ball.

Turning and Shooting

A player who has his back to goal will normally have a defender close by. Offensive players will be marked more tightly the closer they get to the goal.

For a player to be efficient in turning with the ball he must first be familiar with the area behind him. He must know how many defenders are close and at which side they are positioned if they are assigned to mark him. There should also be an awareness of where he is in relation to the goal as this too will have an effect on which direction he turns in. Placing both arms out behind the body will detect which side the defender is overplaying. This is within the rules of the game as long as no holding takes place.

If defenders do overplay one side, the player receiving the ball can attempt to turn with the ball away from the defenders. In doing so, the body can be used as a screen while the effort is made to get the shot away. If a ball is played into the chest, there is still a need for the body to shield the movement, so the player reveals his preference of side at the last moment.

Approach

If a defender is marking tightly, the offensive player can force him back toward his own goal by moving backward to this goal himself. Once the defender has been committed in this direction, the offensive player can check back toward the ball leaving the defender flat-footed. Moving to meet the ball allows an extra yard and a few seconds which the defender finds very difficult to make up. If this defender marks away from his player, there is no need for the offensive player to move his defender away. Good communication between the player making the pass and the player receiving it is important.

Decisions have to be made by the player receiving the ball. The first one concerns the direction he must turn in. The body should be balanced and the foot that is to be used to turn the ball should be prepared and ready to meet it.

Contact

If the player has decided to take the ball with his left foot in order to turn to his left and shoot with his right, the outside of this left foot is the more appropriate surface to use. By using the inside of the foot too much time is spent in turning the body around. Using the outside, very little readjusting of this foot is needed. With one movement the ball can be squeezed to the side and the foot correctly planted. As the player moves to this side the body is used to screen the ball from the ensuing defender. The time that is taken to perform this action is crucial to the intended outcome of the shot. Players should work toward controlling and turning in one swift movement in an effort to improve their shooting capabilities in this area.

Follow-through

The final shot can be classified as the follow-through. It is the final part and finished product of all that has gone before.

Breakaway Shooting

When the attacking player has beaten the final defender or when he has received a ball behind this last player, he must then decide whether to shoot quickly or take the ball around the goalkeeper. Opportunities such as this are not automatic goals. The attitude of the player in possession is paramount in his quest to beat a player who can use his hands. This one moment in a game can separate an average player from a masterful player.

Approach

The player's head must be lifted in order to observe the goalkeeper's position. A goalkeeper who stays on his line presents no real challenge but rather, a clear-cut advantage to the offensive player. An advancing goalkeeper, however, will give this player more to think about as long as he does not rush out with little thought to the situation.

Decide

Decisions have to be made once the goalkeeper's actions have been determined. The two choices are:

- Shoot immediately
- Go around the goalkeeper

The player must now disguise his intentions in an effort to force the goalkeeper into making an error. If the shot is to be taken close to the goal the inside of the foot will achieve greater accuracy; power is not essential.

Going around the goalkeeper requires space beyond the goalkeeper's reach in which to work. Once the goalkeeper has committed himself, the opportunity to finish the task is at hand.

Perform

The final sequence will be to place the ball in the goal with the grace and composure of a world-class performer. Losing concentration at this stage can have a devastating effect, not only on the immediate outcome of the shot, but also on the events that can follow in other aspects of the game.

Once the referee has awarded the goal, it is then, and only then that a player can savor the moment and relish in the glory.

The skill of shooting requires that a player have an attitude which allows him to:

- *Shoot at any time and from any position*
- *Take risks in the attacking third of the field*
- *Perform without fear of failure*

DRILLS

DRILL #1

| PLAYING POSITION: 1ST MAN OFFENSE/SHOOTING |

| COACHING LEVEL: WITHOUT OPPOSITION |

| KEY COACHING POINTS: APPROACH, CONTACT, & FOLLOW-THROUGH |

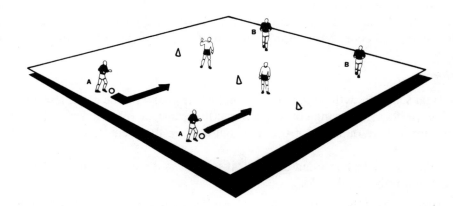

DIAGRAM 5-4

The number of players involved in this drill will determine the organizational setup. Goals can be placed in a straight line across the field with a goalkeeper in each. (See Diagram 5-4.) Two players, A and B, are positioned at either side of the goal. One of these players pushes the ball out in front, then finishes with a shot on goal. If the goalkeeper saves the shot, he turns around and plays the ball out to the other player, who will begin the same routine.

If you are working with beginners a stationary ball can be used in the initial stages. When progress is observed, you can include certain modifications, such as:

- Right or left foot
- Bouncing ball
- Swerve shots

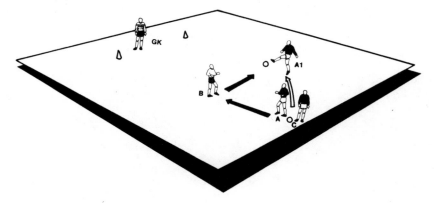

DIAGRAM 5-5

For balls that are played across the field, attention must be directed toward the timing of the shot. Player A passes to player B, as shown in Diagram 5-5. After player B has played the ball to the side, player A moves to meet the pass and finish the movement with a shot as in position A-1. Balls that are played to the left can be struck with the left foot, while balls that are played to the right can be taken with the right foot.

Player C continues the drill after the previous player has completed his move. Player B can maintain his serving position until you decide to make a change.

Balls can be played directly back to the player so as to allow him to strike a ball that is moving into his stride. The drill can also be used with bouncing balls that are chipped up by the server.

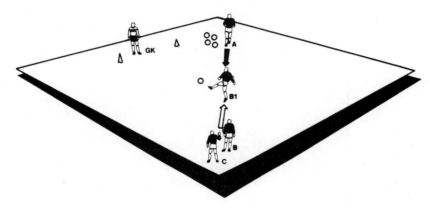

DIAGRAM 5-6

For balls that are played in from the wings, player A has a supply of balls next to him. Player B moves across the goal to receive a pass from player A. (See Diagram 5-6.) He takes a shot at the goal from the position B-1. All players will retrieve their balls after shooting and give them back to the server. You can rotate where necessary. Emphasis should be placed on the:

- Planting of the nonkicking foot
- Vision of the spinning ball
- Good contact

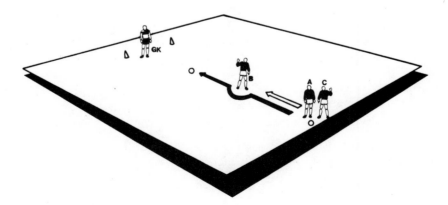

DIAGRAM 5-7

For practice in turning with the ball, player A passes the ball along the ground to player B. (See Diagram 5-7.) Player B controls the ball and turns in one move before getting the shot away quickly. Player A then runs up to take player B's position. Player C begins the drill again. The serve can be varied to practice:

- Thigh control
- Chest control

Instruct the players to think more in terms of a spin than a turn. This will eliminate the unnecessary time loss that often accompanies a slow turn.

DRILL #2

PLAYING POSITION: 1ST MAN OFFENSE/SHOOTING

COACHING LEVEL: PASSIVE OPPOSITION

KEY COACHING POINTS: APPROACH, CONTACT, & FOLLOW-THROUGH

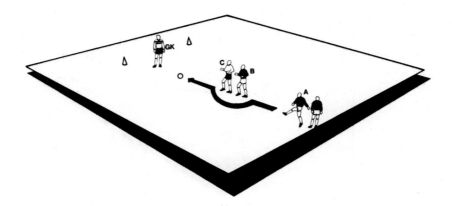

DIAGRAM 5-8

Player A passes the ball to player B. The defensive player C is positioned directly behind player B. Player C can take up a position on either side of player B. If player B is struggling to control and turn in one movement, player C can be positioned further away until some success is attained. Player B can use his body to disguise his intentions by running backward and then checking back to meet the ball. Balls can be served to the chest and the thigh.

DRILL #3

PLAYING POSITION: 1ST MAN OFFENSE/SHOOTING

COACHING LEVEL: POSITIVE OPPOSITION

KEY COACHING POINTS: WHEN & WHERE TO SHOOT

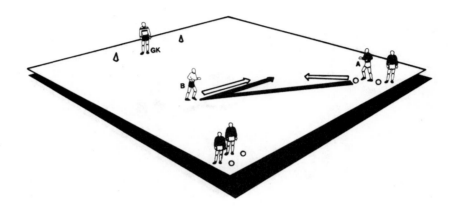

DIAGRAM 5-9

Player A passes to player B, as shown in Diagram 5-9, and then moves to receive the ball back from player B. As soon as this pass is made back to player A, player B gives immediate chase after the ball. A 1 vs. 1 situation is now established, and player A now has to make the decision whether to shoot first-time or to challenge the defender. If player B is slow at moving toward player A, a first-time shot would be more appropriate. If player B is quick to move into position to stop the shot, player A can attempt to beat him.

The drill would continue with another player passing the ball from a different angle. Volleys can be used in the drill, especially side volleys.

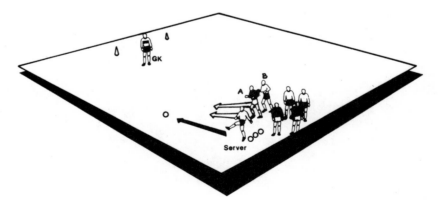

DIAGRAM 5-10

Two players, A and B, position themselves shoulder-to-shoulder facing the goal. (See Diagram 5-10.) A server stands directly behind them and plays a ball to either side. If the ball is played to the side of player A, he becomes the offensive player while player B becomes the defensive player. A 1 vs. 1 situation develops when both players give chase. This will bring out the physical challenge that often occurs when two players compete for the ball.

If the offensive player can take a first-time shot this should be encouraged. If the defender is positioned in a solid defensive stance the ball can be brought inside for a better shooting angle. Two new players will then take up the same position. Right and left foot shots can be taken as can balls that are played in the air.

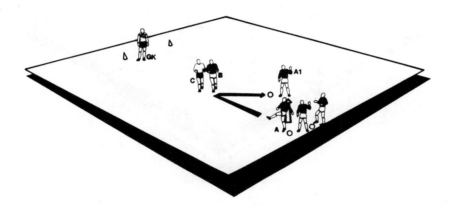

DIAGRAM 5-11

The situation now develops into a 2 vs. 1. More decisions have to be made as teammates start to play a major function in the total performance.

Player A passes the ball into player B who is being tightly marked by player C. (See Diagram 5-11.) Player B may have to move player C backward before checking and coming in to meet the ball. When player A has made the pass he then moves wide to offer support to player B who is attempting to control, turn, and shoot in one movement. If a pass back to player A is more advantageous, this should be used. The defender's positioning will be a major consideration in what the two offensive players attempt. The following should be guiding considerations:

- If player B can turn with the ball around and past the defender this is the first priority.

- If player B can turn and face the defender this is the second priority.

- Use of player A should be the third priority. In the realistic situation of a game, the closer the offense move toward goal, the tighter they are being marked man-to-man. Player A may not be available all the time. Situations will present themselves where player A is in a better shooting position. If this is the case, he should be used quickly.

DRILL #4

| PLAYING POSITION: 1ST MAN OFFENSE/SHOOTING |

| COACHING LEVEL: SMALL-SIDED GAMES |

| KEY COACHING POINTS: WHEN & WHERE TO SHOOT |

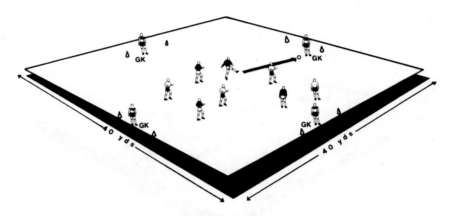

DIAGRAM 5-12

In an area 40 yards x 40 yards four portable goals or four sets of cones are placed in position on the grid lines. A player is used in each of the four goals; these four players can then be rotated as a team with the two groups of four who are active in the center. (See Diagram 5-12.) The object of the game is for either team to score in any goal. The teams are rotated every five minutes. With four goals available to shoot at, numerous chances will be created in which to score. Players from each team will have the opportunity to work extensively at shooting. A small-sided game reinforces the following coaching points that need to be made:

- A shot should be taken quickly.
- A pass should be used if a shot is unavailable.
- Dribbling the ball should be used if neither a shot nor a pass is attainable.

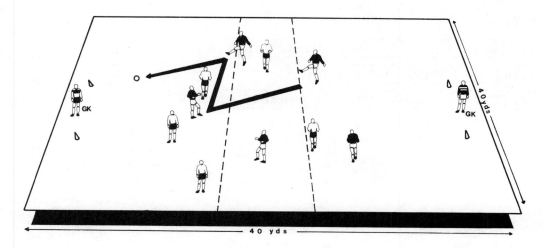

DIAGRAM 5-13

As shown in Diagram 5-13, in an area 40 yards x 40 yards two teams of five will work for two 10-minute halves. Two 15-yard areas in front of each goal are marked off with cones or lines. Once the ball moves into these areas the offensive team has only 10 seconds to take a shot, otherwise possession is given to the other team. The emphasis is placed on players' thinking ahead in order to move swiftly once they are in these restrictive areas. Goalkeepers need to be used in full-size goals.

DRILL #5

| PLAYING POSITION: 1ST MAN OFFENSE/SHOOTING |

| COACHING LEVEL: TEAM TACTICS |

| KEY COACHING POINTS: WHEN & WHERE TO SHOOT |

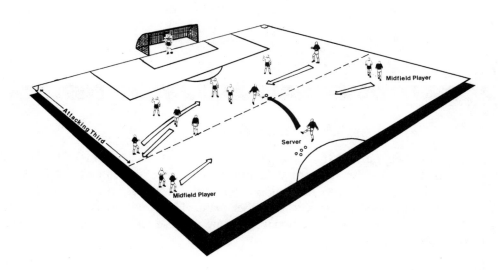

DIAGRAM 5-14

Within one-half of the field the offense has a numerical advantage. A server can play the ball directly in the attacking third of the field or he can pass to either of the two midfield players alongside him. (See Diagram 5-14.) If a pass is made to a midfield player he must compete with a defensive player in the same area. Once the ball is settled in the midfield, a pass is made into the attacking third. The player making the pass can then cross over to support the five attacking players. If the server plays the ball forward into the attacking third, no midfield player is allowed to assist. In this drill, stress that:

- Players must be prepared to take risks.
- Players must make a shot their first priority.

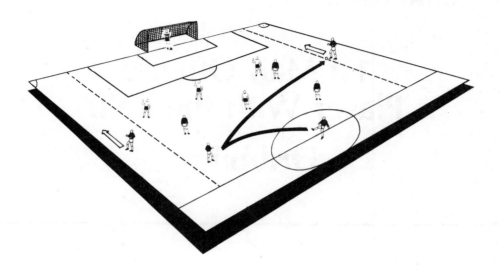

DIAGRAM 5-15

On one-half of the field two defined areas are marked down both wings, 10 yards from the side line, as shown in Diagram 5-15. Only one player from the offensive team can enter each area. The offensive team can begin to build up in the center of the field, but they must finish their buildup with a pass to either wing.

The emphasis is placed on players shooting from passes played in from the wings. If defenders are placed in the restricted areas, there may be an immediate breakdown in the drill if the defender continually wins the ball.

CHAPTER 6

1st Man Offense
Player With the Ball:
Dribbling

COACHING POINTS

To the spectator this part of the game can be as artistic as a well-executed shot on goal. By being able to master the ball with the feet in tight situations a player can place the opposition at a disadvantage through taking away the numerical superiority defenders usually have.

Teaching Creativity

Emphasis in the early stages of learning to dribble with the ball should be placed on a player's acquiring a feel for the ball. Young players need to be encouraged to communicate with the ball using different parts of the foot.

Running with the ball is not the same as dribbling. Possession is more likely to be retained when a player moves down the field unchallenged from an immediate opponent. Close control is required before a player can successfully attempt to beat a defender. Without the immediate threat of having the ball taken away, a player can lift his head to evaluate the next move. Skillful players will allow themselves only a few touches of the ball as they move forward with their heads up. This is a situation where the player allows the ball to do the work.

Of all the individual skills in soccer, dribbling is one of the most difficult to acquire. Armed with this knowledge you realize that to assist in a player's development you have to leave a certain amount of creativity to the player himself.

There are numerous ways to dribble around a defender. Realistically, because of time constraints, these cannot all be coached, yet each exhibits certain fundamental stages which can be understood. These stages will be discussed shortly.

In a 1 vs. 1 situation the emphasis on performance lies with the player in possession. He is the player who can be made to look skilled or unskilled while performing his function. Overplaying the ball is a common fault for beginners. The chances of beating three or four players in one area of the field are remote. Even though dribbling is usually a last resort, certain places on the field are more suitable than others. Players in the attacking third of the field should be encouraged to dribble. There is excessive risk, however, for players who dribble in their own defensive third of the field. It is critical for a team to maintain possession in this defensive area as they begin to build forward.

The three stages that are involved with dribbling are:

- Approach
- Change of direction
- Change of pace

Some players may have problems with all three stages, while others may have problems with only one stage. Only concern yourself with those areas that require work. It is pointless to work on those stages which the player can already perform successfully, unless your practice is designed to be a reinforcing session. Photo Series 6-1 illustrates the three stages of dribbling.

Approach

The ball must be under close control at all times. The movement forward is on a direct path toward the defender. Any sideways movement at this early stage will allow the defender time to adjust his position. Players who move wide in an attempt to beat a defender are only allowing this defender to perform his job successfully.

Defenders must be forced to commit themselves in order for the player in possession to change direction. The speed at which the player approaches the defender must be controlled. If he moves too slowly, he will allow the defender to close him down quickly, thus denying himself any further advancement. If he moves too quickly he increases the chances of losing possession. It is difficult to make a change in direction without having the ball under control. Looking slightly ahead of it allows sight of both the defender and the ball.

Change of Direction

To unbalance a defender the player in possession should react to the commitment of the defender and the need to make the first move. Good defenders are taught to delay a player's forward threat on goal by keeping the player in front of them. A defender can delay this threat for only so long before he must make an effort to win the ball. If the defender challenges too early and commits himself, the player with the ball can then control the situation by responding to this challenge. The defender can also become unbalanced by reacting to the initial move made against him. If this move is convincing, the defender will commit himself to it. The player can again control the situation and move past him.

A change of direction is made slightly outside the defender's reach. If this change of direction is made too early the offensive threat is denied. There are three means of faking out a defender that can be applied collectively or individually. They are by use of the ball, the body, and/or the eyes.

A good defender's vision is directed toward the ball. It is the ball that is the major threat on goal. Defenders who are challenging against the player in possession will react to that ball. Under these circumstances intelligent use of the ball is essential.

When creativity is brought up in coaching, players are often thought of as creating their own individual style. This should never be denied. Dribbling is one skill that a player can use to demonstrate his style and creativity.

Without wanting to stifle a beginner's creativity, some guidelines are in order. The Garrincha Technique is such a guideline. This famous Brazilian winger employed his own style to a move that can be imitated by players today. The Garrincha Technique embodies the use of the ball as the main form of deception.

A player moves toward a defender and at the appropriate distance, just outside tackling range, changes direction of the ball with his right foot by moving it to the left of the midline of the defender's body. As the defender adjusts his weight to that side, the player uses the outside of his right foot to wrap around the ball and push it past him to the exposed side. If the defender does not react to the first touch of the ball then the player can continue down that side instead.

A player can also use his body to unbalance a defender. The shoulders and hips can be effective in moving one way while the foot pushes the ball in the opposite direction. Defenders who direct their visual attention toward the attacker's body are vulnerable to being thrown off balance by this quick, forceful movement. This can be achieved by dipping the shoulders down while turning the hips. A player who uses his body to fake to the left will very often use the outside of his right foot to take the ball past the defender on the side opposite the initial fake. Using the outside of either foot is an effective means to disguise the next move. It requires very little adjustment in order to be performed smoothly.

A defender who watches the feet is just as vulnerable. The feet are effective in unbalancing defenders because they are near the ball. A skillful player can use the feet to distract a defender at a critical point. For example, a player who drags a foot over the ball can move a defender in that direction. The same foot can then move the ball away in the opposite direction.

The eyes are not as effective as the other body parts because defenders rarely look into the eyes of a player with the ball. If a defender does look toward the eyes, a quick glance to one side may work to throw the defender off balance. The emphasis of instruction needs to be directed to the quick movement that produces results.

Change of Pace

A change of direction must be followed immediately by a change of pace. Defenders will recover from mistakes quickly, and therefore it is important for an accelerated phase to accompany the change in direction. Continuing at the same pace will allow the defender to challenge a second time.

A direct route to goal should be taken if there is an opening. This is often determined by the positioning of the supporting defensive players. A player who has beaten his man and then begins to move wide allows the same defender the opportunity to make a recovery run on the goalside of the ball.

If there is space behind a defender, the ball can be played through into this area to allow more speed to be attained without having to deal with controlling it. Attempting to regain control of the ball can hinder progress due to the slowing down by players. If the space in this same area is restricted, close control is essential, yet seldom achieved. It is therefore important to stress that the shot can be taken as quickly as possible especially in the attacking third of the field.

All players should be inventive, creative, and prepared to take risks. The ability to take on and beat other players by dribbling is a positive attribute for a player to possess.

PHOTO SERIES 6-1
DRIBBLING PAST A DEFENDER

(A)
<u>Approach</u>
Movement directly toward a defender

(B)
<u>Approach</u>
Timing the fake

(C)
<u>Change of Direction</u>
Forcing the defender off-balance by faking a movement

(D)
<u>Change of Pace</u>
Accelerating past the defender

In the following 1st Man Offense–Dribbling–Without Opposition–there are drills which require and involve running with the ball. These allow beginners to experience a feel for the ball, while moving around in different directions at different speeds.

DRILL #1

PLAYING POSITION: 1ST MAN OFFENSE/DRIBBLING

COACHING LEVEL: WITHOUT OPPOSITION

KEY COACHING POINTS: APPROACH, CHANGE OF DIRECTION, & CHANGE OF PACE

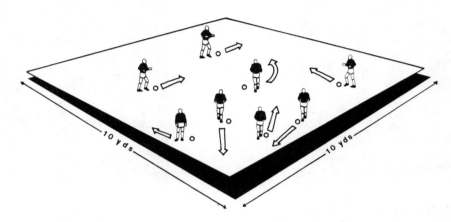

DIAGRAM 6-1

In a defined area of 10 yards x 10 yards a small group of players will each have a ball. (See Diagram 6-1.) On the command of "GO," the players move around freely, keeping close control of the ball. When the coach sounds his whistle a change of direction is required. Different commands can be given out:

- Right foot only
- Left foot only
- Alternate feet
- Outside of the foot only
- Inside of the foot only
- Turning/spinning
- Sole of the foot only

Other tasks can also be given out which have to be performed immediately:

- Right knee touch the ground
- Left knee touch the ground
- Right elbow touch the ground

- Left elbow touch the ground
- Head touch the ground

The idea is for the players to keep the ball moving even while they are performing the tasks. When the coach calls out the command "STOP," all players must find a space before placing one foot on the ball and raising an arm. This will show the coach that the ball is under control.

A simple progression within this drill that young players have fun with is to allow them to kick another player's ball out of the area while protecting their own. When a player's ball is kicked out he must retrieve it and remain outside the area until a winner is determined.

Emphasis is continually placed on:

- Lifting the head to see around
- Keeping the ball within playing distance
- Using different parts of the foot

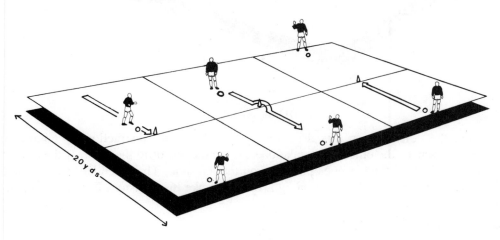

DIAGRAM 6-2

In a 20-yard x 10-yard grid area place a cone on the middle line. One player is positioned at each side of the grid with a ball, as shown in Diagram 6-2. The first player runs toward the cone, dribbling the ball. At the cone he changes the direction of the ball as he fakes a body movement. After moving past the cone he increases his speed to finish at his partner's side. This second player then performs the same movement in the opposite direction. A third player can be introduced to allow the players more rest periods.

In the initial stages of dribbling you should ensure that the players:

- Move toward the cone with the ball under control
- Change direction at the cone
- Change pace after passing the cone

The reason a cone is used in this drill is to allow the players as much contact with the ball as possible. As the drill progresses a defender can take the place of a cone.

DRILL #2

PLAYING POSITION: 1ST MAN OFFENSE/DRIBBLING

COACHING LEVEL: PASSIVE OPPOSITION

KEY COACHING POINTS: APPROACH, CHANGE OF DIRECTION, & CHANGE OF PACE

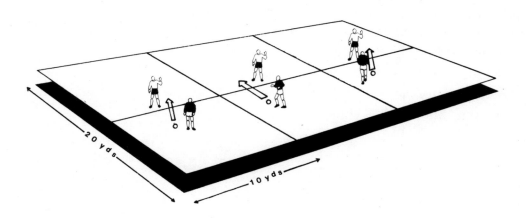

DIAGRAM 6-3

Even though the defenders in this drill are passive they offer distraction by committing themselves one way or the other. They take one step to the left or to the right. If the defender moves to his right the attacker goes past him on the left side. The defender has to time his action so as to give the attacker just enough room to make his decision. Emphasis is placed on:

- A controlled approach
- A decisive change of direction
- An accelerated change of pace

DRILL #3

| PLAYING POSITION: 1ST MAN OFFENSE/DRIBBLING |

| COACHING LEVEL: POSITIVE OPPOSITION |

| KEY COACHING POINTS: WHEN & WHERE TO DRIBBLE |

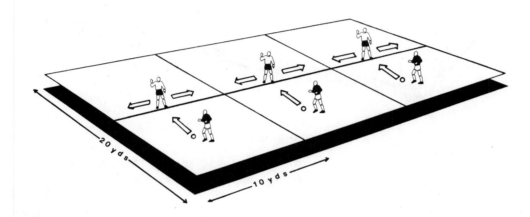

DIAGRAM 6-4

The attacker moves toward the defender positioned on the middle line as in Diagram 6-4. This defender can move only from side to side on the line in an attempt to stop the attacker who must approach the defender, commit him, and then accelerate to the furthest grid line. The emphasis of the drill is on allowing the attacking player to unbalance the defender while first approaching unchallenged.

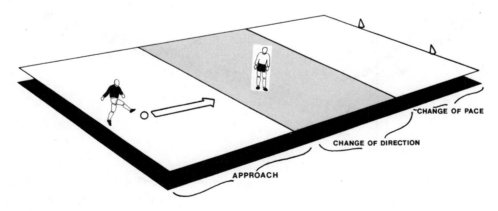

CHANGE OF PACE

CHANGE OF DIRECTION

APPROACH

DIAGRAM 6-5

In three defined areas of 10 yards x 10 yards an offensive player begins from one end grid. (See Diagram 6-5.) The defender is placed in the middle grid and cannot move out of this area. After the player with the ball has approached under control, he must confront the defender. If the offensive player is successful in beating the defender he must continue to accelerate through two cones placed on the back line of the last grid. The three areas that are marked can be used to identify the three stages involved with dribbling.

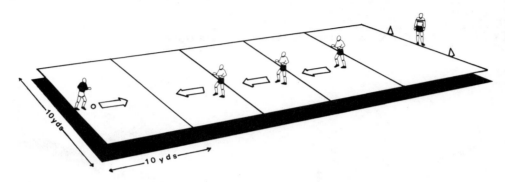

DIAGRAM 6-6

Through a series of 10-yard x 10-yard grids an attacker attempts to beat three defenders in three separate areas. (See Diagram 6-6.) A goalkeeper is added in the final area. Each defender is positioned on the back line of his area and can advance only when the attacker has entered his area. A point is awarded for every defender that is beaten. Three points are additionally awarded if a goal is scored. Close control is essential as the defenders are positioned directly behind each other.

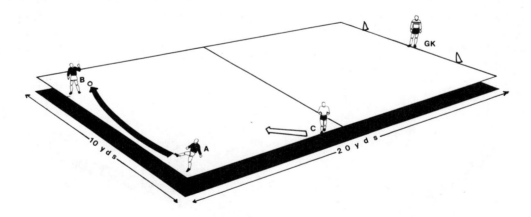

DIAGRAM 6-7

The introduction of an additional attacker brings the drill closer to a game-related situation. Diagram 6-7 shows two attackers, A and B, positioned in the near corners of the first grid. A defender, C, is positioned in one of the other corners in the same grid. A goal is set up in the far grid with a goalkeeper. Player A will pass to player B. Player C then becomes active as soon as player A has released the ball. Player C only challenges in this first grid. You have now created a 2 vs. 1 situation where the emphasis is placed on whether or not the two attacking players should dribble with the ball or pass it. The player in possession must quickly decide which skill is more appropriate.

Stress:

• Close control

• Change of direction

• Change of pace

• When to shoot, pass, or dribble

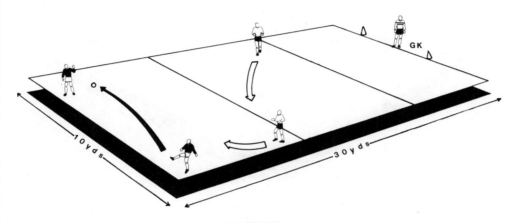

DIAGRAM 6-8

A second defender, as in Diagram 6-8, forces the two attackers to combine their movements. The emphasis is on a 1 vs. 1 situation where the player in possession must be prepared to take risks. The additional attacker supports his teammate from behind before moving forward at the appropriate moment to occupy the second defensive player. A shot can be taken only when at least one defender has been beaten. This encourages players to take on defenders in an effort to finish with a shot.

DRILL #4

PLAYING POSITION: 1ST MAN OFFENSE/DRIBBLING

COACHING LEVEL: SMALL-SIDED GAME

KEY COACHING POINTS: WHEN & WHERE TO DRIBBLE

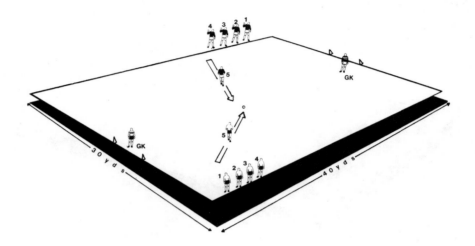

DIAGRAM 6-9

Two teams of five players are positioned on the side lines in their respective halves of the field, 30 yards x 40 yards, as shown in Diagram 6-9. They are close to the corner of the area. Each player is given a number, from one to five. When you call out a number the appropriate player from each team runs out to a ball positioned in the center. These players attempt to dribble it toward the goal they are shooting at.

If a goal is scored a point is awarded. For young players you can replace a point with a letter from the alphabet. When a word has been spelled out by one team, they are the winners.

Progress by calling out more than one number to present a small-sided game. Players must be made aware of their options. They should not be limited to just one skill unless a condition has been imposed.

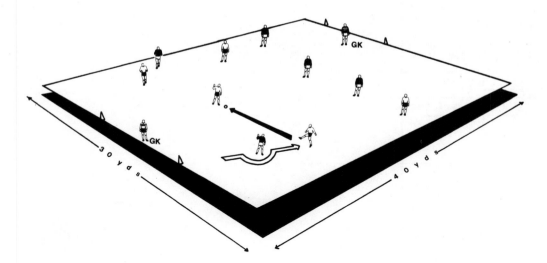

DIAGRAM 6-10

In an area 30 yards x 40 yards, two teams of five outfield players and a goalkeeper play a conditioned game. (See Diagram 6-10.) A player must first beat a defender before he can shoot or pass. This encourages players to attack defenders. After a period of 10-15 minutes unrestricted play can begin. It is in this final segment of the drill that players must now begin to make decisions for themselves.

Even though you are working on the theme of dribbling you must be aware that in the realistic setting of a game, players have to decide whether to shoot, pass, or dribble.

DRILL #5

PLAYING POSITION: 1ST MAN OFFENSE/DRIBBLING

COACHING LEVEL: TEAM TACTICS

KEY COACHING POINTS: WHEN & WHERE TO DRIBBLE

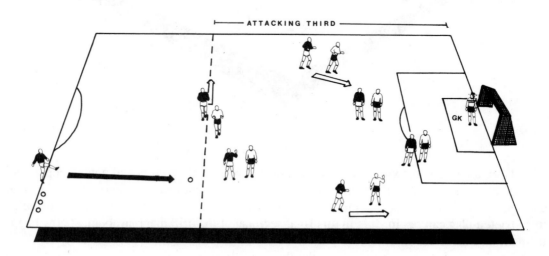

DIAGRAM 6-11

Six offensive players and six defensive players are placed in the attacking third of the field, as in Diagram 6-11. The defenders are instructed to play strict man-to-man defense. A server is positioned around the center circle with a supply of balls. The offensive players attempt to get free in order to receive a pass from the server. When an offensive player has possession he must turn and face his defender before attempting to dribble.

This tight defensive structure will force the offense to create space and utilize it in order to become productive as a team. Stress that there is an element of risk in this movement forward, but it must be accepted in the effort to score.

A progression in this drill is in releasing the defenders of their marking responsibilities. This unrestricted play allows the offense to make constructive decisions.

Selection is narrowed down to:

- Taking a shot if the opportunity presents itself
- Passing the ball if a player is in a more advantageous position
- Dribbling at a defender

The decision to dribble should be made when:

- A shot or a pass is not available.
- There is space directly behind the defender that can be used productively.
- There is help in the form of support from behind.

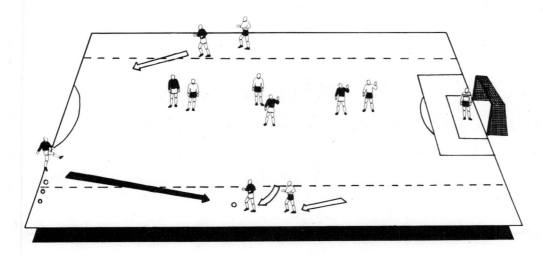

DIAGRAM 6-12

A 6 vs. 6 session is held in one-half of the field. A goalkeeper and server are present. (See Diagram 6-12.) Two lanes are marked off from the goal line up to the halfway line and 15 yards from either sideline. An attacking player competes against a defender in each lane. No other players are allowed in these lanes. The server plays the ball to either one of the attackers in the restrictive areas. A 1 vs. 1 is established down the wing. Only after the defender is beaten can the attacker pass into the middle. The defender can be instructed to allow the attacker to turn before he makes a challenge. The emphasis is placed on:

• Wingers taking on and beating a wing fullback.

Try to be aware that players can produce inventive and creative play only when they are placed in tight, realistic situations. Players must experience these if they are to learn and eventually master the exciting skill of dribbling.

CHAPTER 7

1st Man Offense
Player With the Ball:
Heading

COACHING POINTS

If the game of soccer were played as perfectly as many coaching books envision, then the skill of heading would be practically obsolete. Sound offensive soccer is built on total possession. In theory, the very nature of the game is built around the use of the feet to move the ball. In practice, however, reality sets in and players are confronted with balls that are played in the air. This stems from a tactical move or a poorly hit ball. A ball that is taken down the wing is usually played high across the goal area in an attempt to avoid defensive players who are in the vicinity of the ball.

Offensive and defensive heading is performed with the eventual outcomes being different even though the techniques are very similar. In offensive heading the intention is to direct the ball toward goal or to a teammate, with the emphasis being placed on *accuracy*. Defensive heading requires *power for distance* in an attempt to clear the ball away from the danger area. Controlling the ball with the head is not productive due to the lack of a cushioning effect on the ball.

It is important that you work with players on both techniques regardless of what position they play on the field. Defenders are often found in the attacking third of the field while attackers can be found helping out in the defensive area of the field. Players who acquire all-around ability for different situations are an asset to any team.

Heading—On the Ground

Approach

A player can be moving in stride to head a ball or he can be stationary. It is important in both instances that he is balanced throughout the skill. A wide, stable base is required for the stationary position. One foot is placed in front of the other to allow the upper part of the body to lean backward without the loss of balance. The main force into the ball initiates from the hips and the neck. The arms are placed out from the sides of the body to assist in balancing the movement. The eyes should be focused on the ball throughout its flight while the mouth remains closed. [See Photo Series 7-1(A).]

Contact

The forehead is the correct area used to strike the ball. The player must have confidence in moving his head into the ball. Some players allow the ball to strike the forehead with practically no forward movement. Beginning players are guilty of this because their confidence level is low. With continued encouragement and correct practice they will acquire proficiency in this difficult skill. [See Photo Series 7-1(B).]

Follow-through

The motion of the head and upper body are toward the intended target. This movement will assist with the accuracy needed to direct the ball to its destination.

PHOTO SERIES 7-1
HEADING

HEADING THE BALL ON THE GROUND

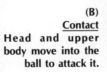

(A)
Approach
Body position prior to heading the ball from a stationary position

(B)
Contact
Head and upper body move into the ball to attack it.

Heading—In the Air

Approach

This is the most difficult element in heading as it requires timing a jumping action. Forward momentum must be converted into upward thrust to allow the body to meet the ball at the most advantageous point in the air. Every player must strive to rise above the opposition if success is to be forthcoming. Players sometimes use a one-footed takeoff to attain this height advantage. It is also easier for a player to take off while he is running in stride. [See Photo Series 7-1(C).]

A one-footed takeoff gives a player more chance of being successful in heading a ball in a direction different from where it was played. A player who is approaching the goal from the left side of the penalty area to head a ball played in from the right, will find it easier to make good contact by his one-footed takeoff.

Do not discourage players who use a two-footed takeoff if the outcome is successful. Some players can attain better balance by taking off on two feet. Defenders who are unchallenged usually acquire this latter approach if they are playing the ball back up the field with power. The arms are used to drive the body upward as well as to help maintain balance. Timing a jump is a difficult part of heading a ball in the air and must therefore be given more time and attention during practice.

Contact

The forehead is again the correct area in striking the ball. Good contact produces a more accurate shot or pass. The eyes must be directed toward the ball.

Follow-through

The head moves toward the target as the body bends at the waist. This allows the legs to balance the action by being placed ahead of the body, similar to a jackknife position. [See Photo Series 7-1(D).]

PHOTO SERIES 7-1
HEADING
(Cont'd)

HEADING THE BALL IN THE AIR

(C)
Approach
The body hangs in preparation to meet the ball

(D)
Follow-through
Body must retain balance throughout the movement

In offensive heading the emphasis is placed on accuracy. In defensive heading the player should concern himself with three priorities:

- Height
- Distance
- Width

A defender must clear the ball away from the area in front of goal. In doing so, he should keep these guidelines in mind: Heading a ball high gives other defenders time to reorganize themselves; heading a ball down toward the ground gives offensive players a second opportunity to get a shot on goal. Also, a ball that is headed for distance denies the opposition any immediate threat on goal; a ball that is played out to the wings prevents the immediate threat of an attack down the middle.

In all heading sessions be aware of the weather conditions and how heavy the ball is. It becomes counterproductive for players to head balls that are too heavy. You will not develop sound players unless their learning is enhanced by enjoyment.

DRILLS

DRILL #1

PLAYING POSITION: 1ST MAN OFFENSE/HEADING

COACHING LEVEL: WITHOUT OPPOSITION

KEY COACHING POINTS: APPROACH, CONTACT, & FOLLOW-THROUGH

DIAGRAM 7-1

For beginners who have not experienced heading, use a foam rubber ball in introductory drills. Players can also begin by heading the ball out of their own hands to acquire a feel for the ball before receiving it from their partners. The following drills can also be used for heading in the air. It is important that players be shown the correct form for an underhand serve. Players can then be divided into pairs 5-10 yards apart. (See Diagram 7-1.) The server throws the ball to his partner who heads back toward the server's feet. This can be repeated ten times before the roles are reversed.

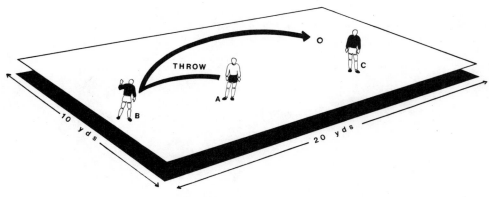

DIAGRAM 7-2

For defensive heading three players are positioned in a straight line, as in Diagram 7-2. Player A serves to player B who heads the ball high over player A to player C. After player C has controlled the header he plays the ball back to player A and the drill continues. The player receiving the header can move wide to create width in the offense. The emphasis is placed on:

- Height
- Distance
- Width

The distance between players can be increased or decreased depending on the proficiency level of the players.

DRILL #2

PLAYING POSITION: 1ST MAN OFFENSE/HEADING

COACHING LEVEL: PASSIVE OPPOSITION

KEY COACHING POINTS: APPROACH, CONTACT, & FOLLOW-THROUGH

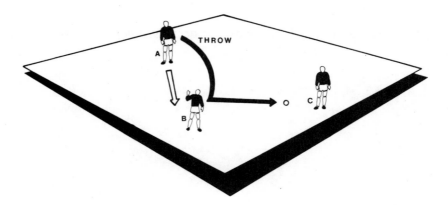

DIAGRAM 7-3

Three players are positioned in a triangle, as in Diagram 7-3. Player A throws the ball to player B. Player B heads the ball down to player C. Immediately after player A has served the ball he runs in toward player B and distracts him. The drill continues with player C serving into player A who has returned to his original position. Player C then makes his run toward player A.

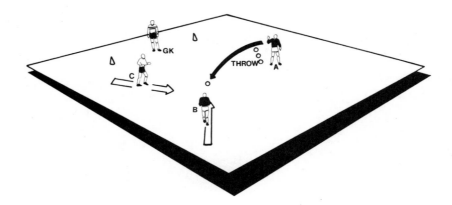

DIAGRAM 7-4

Directing a header toward goal usually requires movement across the face of the goal to meet the ball. (See Diagram 7-4.) Player A serves the ball to player B who is moving toward the server. Player C is positioned on the back post of a portable goal or cones. As soon as player A has released the ball, player C begins his challenging run. Players will become fatigued unless they are rotated frequently.

DRILL #3

| PLAYING POSITION: 1ST MAN OFFENSE/HEADING |

| COACHING LEVEL: POSITIVE OPPOSITION |

| KEY COACHING POINTS: WHEN & WHERE TO HEAD |

If the ball can be served correctly with the feet then this should be encouraged.

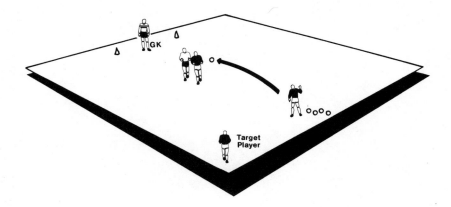

DIAGRAM 7-5

A goalkeeper is positioned between two cones. An attacker and defender are positioned close together 10-15 yards away from goal, as shown in Diagram 7-5. A server plays a high ball in the air toward both players. If the attacker can reach the ball first he plays it back down to the server's feet. Once the server has the ball under control a 2 vs. 1 can be set up toward goal. If the defender reaches the ball first he should aim for a target player wide of the server.

Points can be awarded for every goal scored or every time the target player receives the defensive pass. Emphasis must be placed on:

- Timing when heading in the air
- Aggressive movement to win the ball

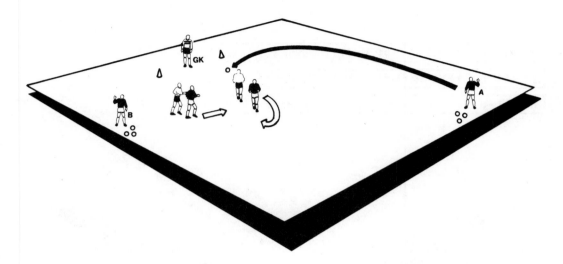

DIAGRAM 7-6

Two servers are positioned with a supply of balls. One server is in a central position while the other is out on the wing. (See Diagram 7-6.) Two attackers are closely marked by two defenders in front of the goal. The serves are rotated and varied. The attackers must coordinate their movements in an attempt to win the ball and take a shot on goal. The first touch by either attacker must be a header. Both defenders should destroy the play by moving quickly to meet the ball.

The attacker who heads the ball first must attempt to play it down to the feet of his teammate. Receiving balls from all angles will familiarize players with their functions under different and demanding circumstances.

The attacking players must:

- Combine their movements
- Be first to the ball
- Perform the skill with great accuracy
- Create a second play

The defending players must:

- Combine their movements
- Cover the attacking players
- Be first to the ball
- Destroy the play

DRILL #4

PLAYING POSITION: 1ST MAN OFFENSE/HEADING

COACHING LEVEL: SMALL-SIDED GAME

KEY COACHING POINTS: WHEN & WHERE TO HEAD

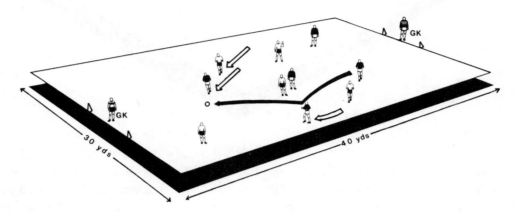

DIAGRAM 7-7

In an area 40 yards x 30 yards, two teams of six compete in a conditioned game of Throw–Head–Catch, as illustrated in Diagram 7-7. The game begins with a player holding the ball until a teammate is available to receive his throw. The player receiving this ball must head it to another teammate who then catches the ball and begins the sequence again. Once the ball is in a player's hands he cannot move with the ball. Players can intercept a badly headed ball but they cannot interfere with a ball that has just been thrown. A goal can be scored only with the head. The emphasis is placed on:

- Quality heading
- An awareness of other players
- Timing both runs and jumps

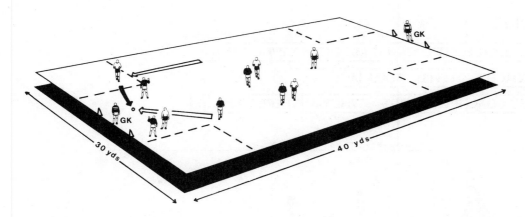

DIAGRAM 7-8

A small-sided game is played in an area 40 yards x 30 yards. Four small grids of 10 yards x 10 yards are marked in the corners. (See Diagram 7-8.) An attacking player in possession of the ball is the only player allowed to enter this area. Once he has entered this area he cannot be challenged. The ball is then crossed over from this area toward the goal. Any ball that goes out of play, that is, throw-in, corner kick, goal kick, can be put back into play only by a player's receiving the ball to his head.

Although an attacking player has time to cross the ball from the corner areas unchallenged, he must still attempt to play an early ball if teammates are available. A defense will be allowed to recover quickly if this attacking player delays for too long.

DRILL #5

PLAYING POSITION: 1ST MAN OFFENSE/HEADING

COACHING LEVEL: TEAM TACTICS

KEY COACHING POINTS: WHEN & WHERE TO HEAD

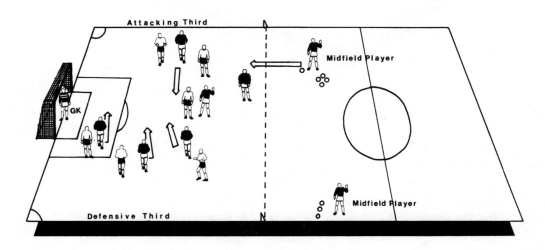

DIAGRAM 7-9

Two midfield players are positioned close to both sidelines with a supply of balls, as in Diagram 7-9. Six offensive players and six defensive players are in the final third of the field. One of the midfield players makes a run with the ball down the wing into this attacking third. He then plays the ball across for the attacking players to meet and play toward goal. The defenders must destroy this by clearing the ball. The ball can be worked down both wings.

The player crossing the ball must:

- Move quickly down the wing
- Lift his head to view the field
- Play the ball early if players are open

The offensive players must:

- Communicate with each other as to who is moving where
- Be first to meet the ball with a quick, well-timed burst of speed
- Be physically and mentally aggressive in the effort to be first to the ball
- Realize their options as they approach the ball

The defensive players must:

- Mark the offensive players quickly

- Be first to the ball
- Be physically and mentally aggressive in the effort to be first to the ball
- Know their priority—Destroy the play quickly

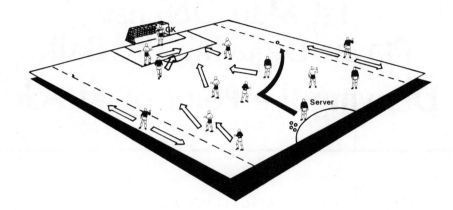

DIAGRAM 7-10

On one-half of a field a server is positioned close to the center circle with a supply of balls. (See Diagram 7-10.) He can play the ball to any offensive player who in turn must attempt to pass into one of the two lanes that have been marked off down the wings. An unchallenged attacker is placed in these lanes; his function is to cross the ball into the middle of the goal area where other offensive players can be found. Depending on which part of offensive heading you are working on, players can head directly for goal or they can head the ball down to a player in a more realistic shooting position.

You can create a more realistic situation by introducing a defender on both sides of the field to challenge this lane player. The reason this defender is not placed in the lane earlier, is to give the winger time to play the ball across. The drill is designed for heading and includes the correct balance of challenging players against the offense. Immediate pressure should not be placed on this wing player as his primary function is to play a ball across that can be headed.

You should gauge the success or failure that the winger is experiencing and adapt accordingly.

The emphasis must be placed on:

- A correct service into the penalty area
- Players communicating with each other
- Players combining their movements to create and utilize space
- Players responding to and acting on the type of service received
- Players attacking the ball in order to be first to the ball

The timing and angle of runs will be discussed in the section on the 3rd Man Offense. They are an integral part of the game, but for the purpose of clarity they have been explained later.

CHAPTER 8

1st Man Defense
Player Delaying the Ball:
Denying the Point of Attack

COACHING POINTS

In developing the concept of soccer as a game of opposites, you now begin to work on the area of defense that denies any immediate threat from the point of attack. The 1st Man Defense is the player who will attempt to prevent any such threat. He is usually the player closest to the ball and is the most important individual on defense.

The sequence of skills that the 1st Man Offense is attempting to use will be denied in similar order by the 1st Man Defense. They are:

- Intercepting any pass from the offense
- Preventing the 1st Man Offense from turning
- Stopping an immediate shot
- Stopping the forward pass
- Stopping the forward dribble

Denying an offensive player space, time, and options reduces his effectiveness in performing his roles. The 1st Man Defense has more influence and opportunity to do this than does any other player on the field. It is his presence and actions that will immediately affect the forward offensive movement. There are three main factors associated with the 1st Man Defense. They are:

- Approach
- Angle
- Distance

Approach

The approach is dependent upon where the 1st Man Offense is on the field in relation to the goal, and also upon the position the 1st Man Defense finds himself in in relation to the ball. All positional play on the field is dependent on where the ball and the goal are located.

Speed of Approach

The defender will usually have to cover a lot of ground in an effort to close down the 1st Man Offense. His approach should be as fast and controlled as possible to make up as much ground as possible while the ball is being played from one player to another. If the pass can be intercepted this should be done. Being first to the ball gives a defender automatic possession from which a counterattack can develop. The 1st Man Defense should not approach too fast over the last few yards because this gives him insufficient time to adjust his direction should the attacker move with the ball at the last moment. If the defender does not react quickly in closing down the player, the attacker can advance forward with a shot, pass, or dribble.

Preventing the 1st Man Offense From Turning

The speed of approach is also important in preventing any direct threat on goal from developing. An attacking player who is forced to play the ball with his back to goal has little opportunity to move forward. If he elects to hold and shield the ball, defenders will be able to recover and deny him space in which to work. Or he can play the ball away from the goal which benefits the defense by denying his team the opportunity to strike quickly.

Angle

Positioning Between Ball and Goal

Not only must a defender be capable of moving at speed but he should be proficient in moving into line between the ball and the goal. If the defender can intercept the pass then his angle of approach is into the line of the pass. (See Diagram 8-1.)

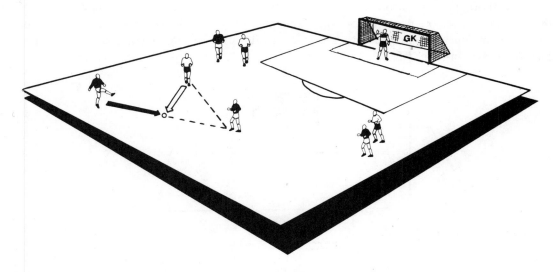

DIAGRAM 8-1

If the defender can reach his opponent as he receives the pass then the angle of approach is directly toward this player. (See Diagram 8-2.) This also assists in preventing the player in possession from turning.

DIAGRAM 8-2

The 1st Man Defense should not always go directly toward the 1st Man Offense. There are occasions where he must first prevent a shot from being taken by quickly positioning himself in a direct line between the ball and the goal. There must be a balance between:

- Positioning on this line as quickly as possible
- Positioning close to the 1st Man Offense as quickly as possible

If the 1st Man Defense simply moves into the line, he may allow the attacker time in which to shoot, pass, or dribble. If he moves in a direct path to the player, he may again allow the attacker to shoot, pass, or dribble. The correct approach would be to balance both functions by curving around into the line, while still closing down the attacker. (See Diagrams 8-3 through 8-5.)

DIAGRAM 8-3
By moving directly onto the line between the ball and the middle of the goal, the 1st Man Defense is allowing the attacker valuable time in which to advance.

DIAGRAM 8-4

By moving directly toward the attacker, the 1st Man Defense is allowing the attacker valuable time in which to advance. There is no protection being given to the goal.

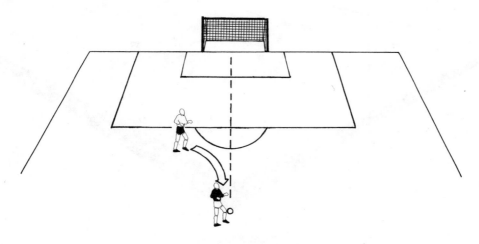

DIAGRAM 8-5

Because of the angle taken up in the approach run, the 1st Man Defense is now denying the attacker time and space in which to perform. The defender moves toward the attacker and still covers the most direct route to goal.

Forcing the Play

When a defender prepares to force the 1st Man Offense in a certain direction he becomes predictable in his movements. This movement can still prove purposeful, however, as it is the outcome and not the intention that is of primary importance. There are many tactical reasons which require a defender to choose one means of forcing a player over another. Coaches differ in their tactical plays, yet there are three major directions which are forced on the 1st Man Offense:

- Channeling down the wings
- Funneling into the middle
- Applying pressure across the field

Channeling Down the Wings

The main reasons that a defender forces a player down the wings are:

- To deny ball possession in front of goal
- To force a predictable play
- To allow defenders to seal off valuable working space

A player who has possession on the wings has very little opportunity to shoot on goal; there are limited opportunities for him to pass the ball. If a defender intends to force a player wide, then his angle of approach is to cut off the inside path of this player. (See Diagram 8-6.)

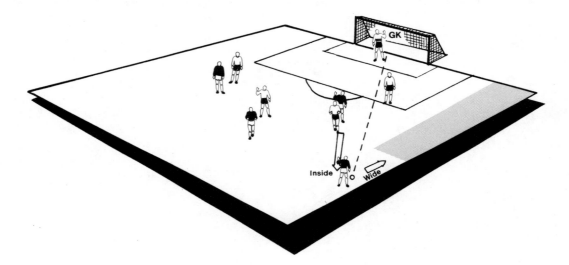

DIAGRAM 8-6

Channeling out toward the wings, the defender overplays the inside path of the attacker to force him wide.

Funneling Into the Middle

There are two reasons why a defender allows an attacker into the middle of the field:

- The attacker's strength is to play down the wing.
- A compact defense is organized inside.

This play is shown in Diagram 8-7.

If the 1st Man Defense has elected to force his player inside because of the threat from down the wing, a covering player must assist this movement. This will be discussed under the 2nd Man Defense. This is not the normal procedure, as any player moving inside is a threat, regardless of where his strengths and weaknesses lie.

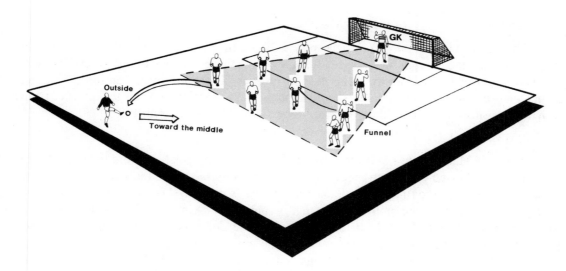

DIAGRAM 8-7

The 1st Man Defense forces the attacker into the middle of the field where a group of defenders has sealed off the vital space through their funneling positions.

A compact defense will cause confusion for an attacker due to the restriction in time and space in which to work. This is a frequently used tactic when a total defense recovers back into a funneled area in front of goal. The angle that the 1st Man Defense moves along is intended to overplay the outside space.

Another instance of forcing a player inside occurs in the attacking third when a player bringing the ball out from his own goal area is forced back into the middle. If possession is lost, it becomes more productive for the team winning possession to regain the ball in the middle of the field.

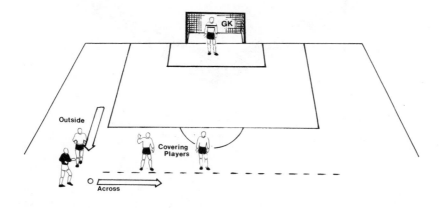

DIAGRAM 8-8

The defender is forcing the attacker across the field by denying him access to either a forward or a wide movement.

Applying Pressure Across the Field

The defense continually keeps the play in front in order to reduce the threat of any penetration into the heart of the defense. Teams become more effective in this procedure once a covering player is made aware of his responsibilities. These are discussed under the 2nd Man Defense. The 1st Man Defense should adopt a position which prevents the attacker from moving forward down the middle, or wide to the wing. (See Diagram 8-8.)

Recovery Run

If the 1st Man Defense is beaten, the 2nd Man Defense usually covers for him. There are certain circumstances which require the 1st Man Defense to give immediate chase after the attacker. This is required if no defensive support is present. The recovery run must be performed quickly to make up the ground that is continually being lost. The angle of this run must be goalside of the attacker. To achieve this, the defender moves to the side of the attacker's body that is closest to the middle of the goal.

A challenge should not be made alongside the attacker unless the ball can be played out of bounds. This is possible when the defender is close to the sideline. The 1st Man Defense must ensure that he takes up a position that will delay the attacker. He does this by placing his body in a direct line between the ball and the goal. This will assist him in recovering his footing as he begins to run backward. (See Diagram 8-9.)

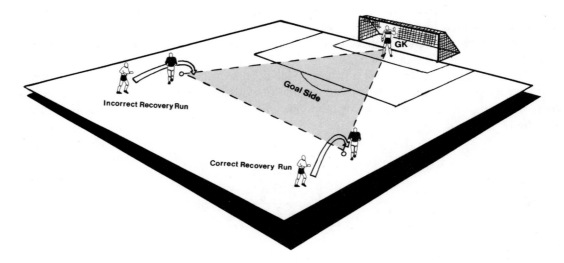

DIAGRAM 8-9

By making his recovery run on the goal side of the attacker, the 1st Man Defense forces the attacker away from the goal.

Distance

The 1st Man Defense must decide how close to position himself to the 1st Man Offense; this depends on whether he is attempting to prevent a shot, a pass, or a dribble. If he is preventing a shot or pass he should be positioned closer than if preventing a dribble. A player can balance all the requirements of good defensive positioning by adopting a position two yards from the ball. This will partially block an attacker's forward vision, restricting the opportunities previously available to him.

One of the most important functions performed by the positioning of the 1st Man Defense is forcing the attacker to give up possession by the immediate pressure imposed on the ball. This does not force the defender to commit himself by tackling; instead, the defender is more effective by staying on his feet and forcing the attacker to give up the ball through intimidation. (See Diagrams 8-10 and 8-11.)

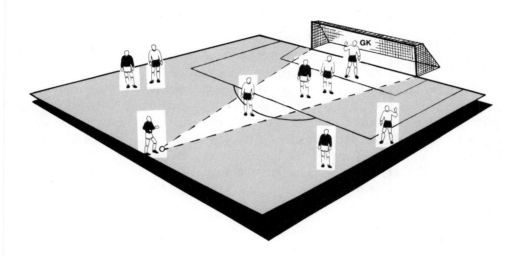

DIAGRAM 8-10
The 1st Man Defense fails to close down the 1st Man Offense, thus allowing shooting and passing opportunities to emerge.

DIAGRAM 8-11
The 1st Man Defense closes down the 1st Man Offense, denying him any forward movement into the vital area.

Body Position

Closing down an attacker requires the defender to bend his body from the knees in a sideways position. Once he is positioned low, he can shuffle his feet backward. The feet should not cross over each other, however, as this will cause loss of balance. A stable position allows:

- Closer vision of the ball
- The correct balance
- A low center of gravity, which is helpful in performing a solid tackle

The 1st Man Defense forces his body in the direction that he wants the 1st Man Offense to move. This allows the attacker slightly more space on one side in which to work, but this side will be the one that the defender is trying to expose.

The defender's attention must be directed toward the ball and not toward the attacker. If the defender is preventing the attacker from turning with the ball, he should acquire a low body position behind the attacker, but he must still give the ball top priority. He should be able to observe it through the attacker's legs if the defender's position is low enough. If the defender can place his foot between the attacker's legs, he will increase his chances of winning the ball. This is more productive than committing to one side of the attacker's body, which can be self-defeating if the attacker moves off in the opposite direction.

Timing

While watching the ball a defender must be patient and force the attacker to make the next move. If the defender makes a predictable tackle in a no-win situation, the attacker will react accordingly. Defenders need not—indeed, should not—commit themselves when they are unsure. The correct time at which to make a tackle is:

- When the attacker looks down toward the ball.
- When the ball is pushed too far outside the reach of the attacker. This can be encouraged when a defender fakes an intended move for the ball. By initiating the first move, the attacker may "take the bait" and commit himself.

By remaining on his feet, a defender enhances his chances of delaying the attack and possibly winning the ball.

Tackling

There is a natural aggression in all players which, if harnessed correctly, can be a productive means of winning the ball. When the appropriate situation presents itself, a defender can attempt to regain possession by tackling. Tackling is, however, a last resort as it involves a certain amount of risk on the defender's part. Giving an attacker a direct route to goal by overreacting, is counterproductive to any phase of a sound defense. Tackling can be a productive play if it is technically correct and used at the right time.

Any means of stealing the ball away from an opponent can be classified as tackling, if it is performed within the rules of the game. Some coaches stress one form of tackling over another depending on the area of the field. A player running with the ball down the wing is usually denied any further movement by a defender's slide tackle. Other areas of the field require a block tackle to be performed. This latter tackle is the one more frequently used as it is carried out with the body in balance. The proper technique for a block tackle is as follows:

- The body is lowered with the tackling leg bent at the knee. The foot is turned outward and locked firm. The striking area is the inside of the foot.
- The nontackling leg aids in the balancing of the body by bending at the knee. The nontackling foot is placed behind the ball.
- The body weight then moves through the ball after the tackling foot has begun to make contact with the middle of the ball.

DRILLS

DRILL #1

PLAYING POSITION: 1ST MAN DEFENSE/DELAY

COACHING LEVEL: WITHOUT OPPOSITION

KEY COACHING POINTS: APPROACH, ANGLE, & DISTANCE

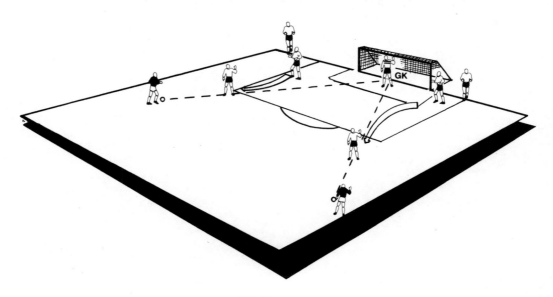

DIAGRAM 8-12

Two groups of defending players work on both sides of the goal, as shown in Diagram 8-12. Two attacking players are positioned with a ball at different angles from the goal. A defending player runs from his group and closes down the attacking player. The groups can be rotated. The emphasis is placed on:

- A fast, controlled approach
- Moving on the line between the middle of the goal and the ball

The ball is now played into an attacker who has his back to goal. (See Diagram 8-13.) The defender must close him down quickly while making up ground as the ball is being passed. You can also work on the defender's intercepting the ball while it is being played. The emphasis is placed on:

- Intercepting the ball
- Preventing the attacker from turning with the ball

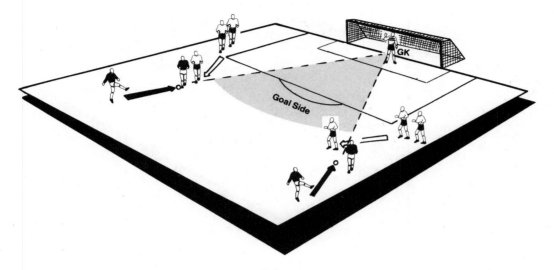

DIAGRAM 8-13

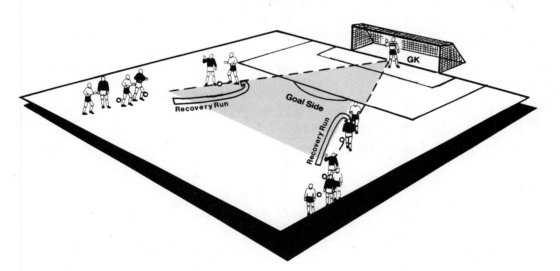

DIAGRAM 8-14

An attacking player moves slowly toward the goal. A defender who is positioned behind him moves to make a recovery run in order to close him down. (See Diagram 8-14.) The speed of the attacker can be varied as can the distance of the defender from the attacker. Once the defender is in position, the drill can begin again with two different players. The emphasis is placed on:

- Moving quickly on the recovery run
- Staying on the goal side of the attacker
- Closing down the attacker

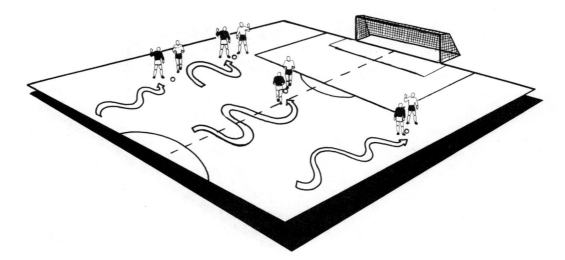

DIAGRAM 8-15

An attacker and a defender move down the field, as in Diagram 8-15. The defender is already in a delay position as the attacker moves the ball from side to side. The defender must adjust his body position constantly as he attempts to keep the attacker away from the middle of the field. Once the attacker moves across the center of the goal the defender forces him toward the opposite wing. The speed at which the attacker moves can be varied. The emphasis is placed on:

- Maintaining a low and balanced body position
- Correct shifting of the feet and body
- Maintaining a close distance of 2 yards

DRILL #2

PLAYING POSITION: 1ST MAN DEFENSE/DELAY

COACHING LEVEL: PASSIVE OPPOSITION

KEY COACHING POINTS: APPROACH, ANGLE, & DISTANCE

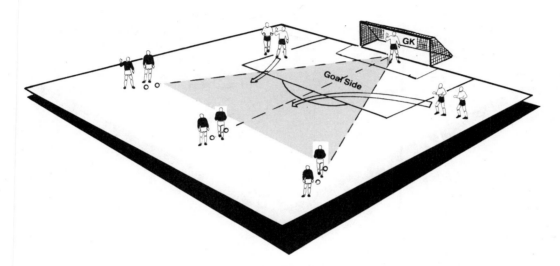

DIAGRAM 8-16

An attacker moves toward the goal as a defender approaches on the correct angle and then begins to delay him over a certain distance. (See Diagram 8-16.) The defenders can be rotated around from different starting positions. The attacking player varies his speed before finishing with a shot. The level of involvement from the defender is limited. Tackling can be introduced gradually.

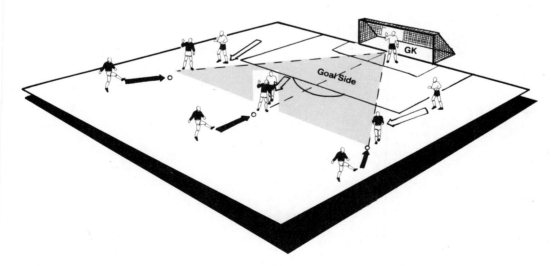

DIAGRAM 8-17

A ball is played into an attacker who is positioned with his back to goal, as shown in Diagram 8-17. A challenging defender moves toward him in an attempt to prevent him from turning with the ball. You may require that the defender intercept the ball if at all possible. This will depend on the pace of the pass and the position of the defender. If the attacker turns with the ball, the defender should delay quickly. Defenders can be rotated.

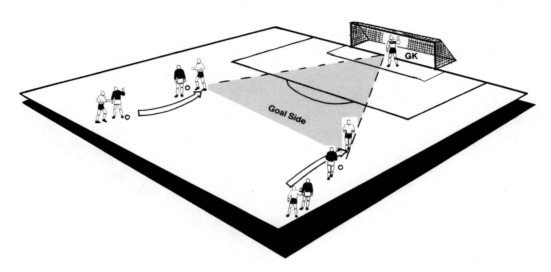

DIAGRAM 8-18

The defender chases after the attacker on the goal side. (See Diagram 8-18.) As soon as he is in position a delaying tactic can be applied. The defender's presence should be felt as he denies the attacker any further advancement. The speed of the attacker can be varied.

DRILL #3

| PLAYING POSITION: 1ST MAN DEFENSE/DELAY |

| COACHING LEVEL: POSITIVE OPPOSITION |

| KEY COACHING POINTS: APPROACH, ANGLE, & DISTANCE |

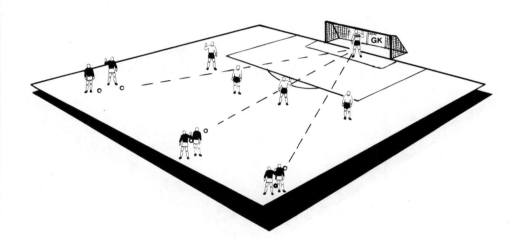

DIAGRAM 8-19

Defenders are randomly positioned anywhere around the goal area, as shown in Diagram 8-19. Attacking players bring the ball toward the goal. The defender who is closest to the ball and in the most advantageous position to deny the attacker, approaches quickly and at the correct angle. The attacker must attempt to score a goal while the defender introduces sound delay with productive tackling.

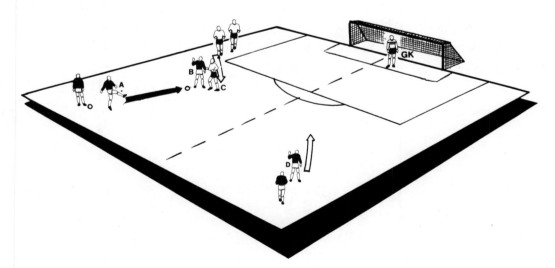

DIAGRAM 8-20

Player A passes the ball into player B who has his back to goal. (See Diagram 8-20.) Player C prevents player B from turning. Player D assists player B by moving forward to develop a 2 vs. 1. If the ball is played from player B over to player D, the defending player C must balance both threats on goal. The drill can begin from different positions. The emphasis is placed on:

- Balancing both threats
- Reacting to the ball

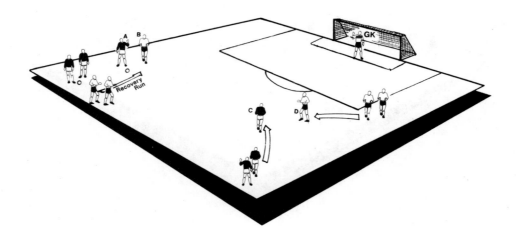

DIAGRAM 8-21

A progression is made to a 2 vs. 2 including a recovery run. (See Diagram 8-21.) Player A moves forward with the ball while player B gives immediate chase. Players C and D assist their respective teammates by moving into supporting positions. Be concerned with the delaying tactics of the 1st Man Defense. The defender who is closest to the ball must react to the immediate threat. Communication is important for the effective positioning of the defense. The emphasis is placed on:

- Deciding when to pressure and when to support
- Deciding when to tackle and when to delay

DRILL #4

PLAYING POSITION: 1ST MAN DEFENSE/DELAY

COACHING LEVEL: SMALL-SIDED GAME

KEY COACHING POINTS: WHEN & WHERE TO DELAY

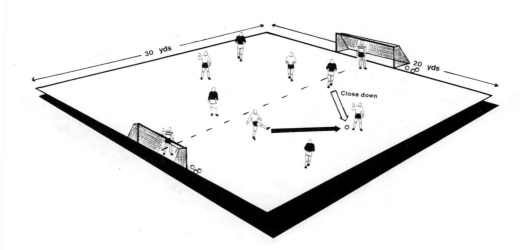

DIAGRAM 8-22

Goals are placed in an area 30 yards x 20 yards. A 5 vs. 5 situation is arranged, with two goalkeepers acting as servers. The coach conditions the game by asking the defender closest to the ball and in an advantageous position to quickly close down the attacker in possession. The defender can call "ball" loud and clear as he approaches the attacker. He must then delay as long as possible without allowing a shot on goal. The emphasis is placed on:

- Reacting quickly to the ball
- Delaying in balance
- Effective communication

DRILL #5

PLAYING POSITION: 1ST MAN DEFENSE/DELAY

COACHING LEVEL: TEAM TACTICS

KEY COACHING POINTS: DESIGNED TOWARD THE TACTIC

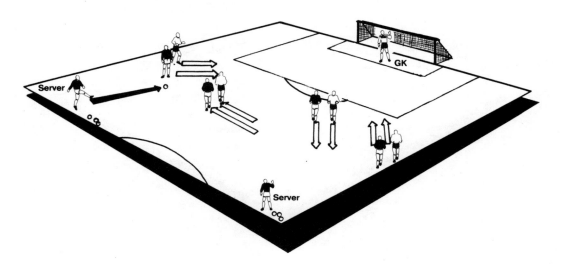

DIAGRAM 8-23

Two servers play balls into five attacking players who are marked in a man-to-man defense. The attackers must try to create space to receive a pass while the defenders prevent them from turning with the ball. If an attacking player cannot move forward once in possession, he can play the ball back to the servers. The defenders can also work on intercepting the ball. The emphasis is placed on:

- Preventing the attacker from turning with the ball
- Early decisions on whether to intercept the pass or prevent the turn
- Effective communication

CHAPTER 9

2nd Man Offense:
Player Supporting
the 1st Man Offense

COACHING POINTS

Reasons for Offering Support

The 2nd Man Offense is the player who is directly supporting the 1st Man Offense from behind. A team cannot always move forward with the ball and therefore it becomes necessary for a pass to be made behind. This allows for the exploration of other offensive opportunities.

A defense rarely marks offensive players positioned behind the ball unless they are playing a strict man-to-man defense. This allows the 2nd Man Offense valuable time in which to make a decision once he receives a pass. The support that this 2nd Man Offense offers will allow the 1st Man Offense a sure and safe pass if needed.

Types of Support

The 2nd Man Offense is responsible to the 1st Man Offense in three ways:

- *Attacking possibilities.* His position may allow him to view other areas of the field and observe situations developing which the 1st Man Offense cannot see.
- *Defensive possibilities.* Should the 1st Man Offense lose possession of the ball the 2nd Man Offense adjusts his function to that of 1st Man Defense immediately.
- *Mental reassurance.* His reassurance, both verbally and positionally, allows the 1st Man Offense to go forward on a dribble.

This supporting play of the 2nd Man Offense is functional throughout the game as a means to assist the 1st Man Offense. Tactically he can be effective in his movements away from this position by making constructive runs to threaten the defensive space beyond the ball. It must be understood by other offensive players that once such a run takes place, another attacker must slot into the vacated 2nd Man position.

There are three factors that should be taught concerning the positioning of the 2nd Man Offense in relation to the 1st Man Offense:

- Distance
- Angle
- Communication

Distance From 1st Man Offense

The distance of the 2nd Man Offense is very often determined by where the ball is positioned on the field.

In the attacking third, the distance is between 5 and 10 yards due to the restriction on space and time. This 2nd Man Offense must offer immediate assistance in tight situations.

In the middle third, the distance is between 10 and 15 yards due to the availability of more space. This area of the field is often referred to as the transitional area from offense to defense and from defense to offense. The presence of the 2nd Man Offense provides a series of outlets which can change the direction of play in a very pronounced manner.

In the defensive third, the distance is between 10 and 30 yards. The threat from the opposition determines the exact distance. If there is little chance of immediate pressure, a wide-angled support position can be used. This offers the 1st Man Offense the opportunity to switch the play in the opposite direction. In this position the 2nd Man Offense is used as the pivot player and the ball is played through him as it passes across the field. Playing a long, cross-field pass can prove costly in the defensive third.

When a defensive team is applying immediate pressure, the 2nd Man Offense must take up a closer position to the 1st Man Offense. This provides a quick and easy outlet if the threat of losing possession gets stronger.

A balance should be achieved between being too close and too far away. If the 2nd Man Offense is too close, congestion occurs around the immediate area of the ball. Other players are drawn in like bees to honey. This is very often the case with young players who swarm around the ball in an effort to touch it. This congestion can also restrict the amount of time available to the 2nd Man Offense should he receive a pass. He will be forced to rush the pass which, in turn, very often leads to a loss of possession.

If the 2nd Man Offense is too far away, then the pass from the 1st Man Offense has a chance of being intercepted. The defense is also given the opportunity to reorganize quickly as the pass is being played away from the space alongside and behind them.

The 2nd Man Offense has a defensive function should the 1st Man Offense lose the ball. If there is too much distance between these two players and the ball is lost, there is more ground for the 2nd Man Offense to cover if his role switches to that of 1st Man Defense. (See Diagrams 9-1 through 9-4.)

Angle From 1st Man Offense

The angle varies according to the position of the opposition. This best angle between the 1st and 2nd Man Offense is one that allows a pass to be made and received with relative ease. The best angle is usually at 45 degrees from the 1st Man Offense on the goal side.

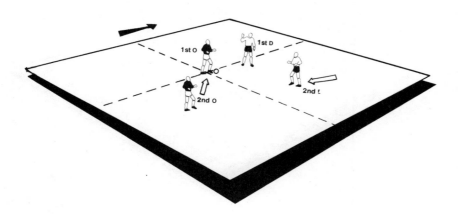

DIAGRAM 9-1

Congestion can occur in the immediate area surrounding the ball if the 2nd Man Offense is positioned too close to the 1st Man Offense.

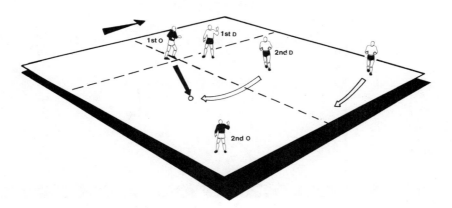

DIAGRAM 9-2

The pass can be intercepted if played over a long distance to the 2nd Man Offense. The remaining defensive players also have time to reorganize quickly.

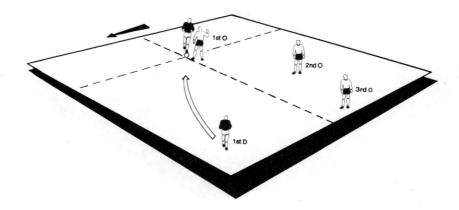

DIAGRAM 9-3

If possession is regained by the defense, the previous 2nd Man Offense is now required to move across in the role of 1st Man Defense. Valuable time is lost when this player has to cover more ground than he should in closing down the play.

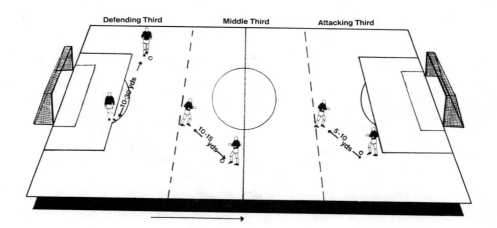

DIAGRAM 9-4

The approximate distance between the 2nd Man Offense and the 1st Man Offense should be different in different areas of the field.

If the 2nd Man Offense is directly behind the 1st Man Offense there is no advantage in his position because the range of passing possibilities is reduced, the 1st Man Offense has restricted vision of his support, and there is limited vision of the field. (See Diagram 9-5.)

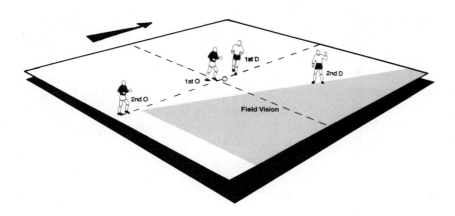

DIAGRAM 9-5

The 2nd Man Offense should not be positioned directly behind the 1st Man Offense, because this restricts vision and passing possibilities.

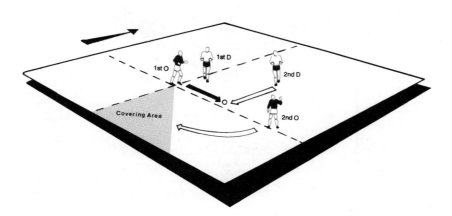

DIAGRAM 9-6

The 2nd Man Offense should not be positioned directly alongside the 1st Man Offense. The distance to be covered is too great and the passes become easier to intercept.

If the 2nd Man Offense is positioned directly alongside the 1st Man Offense there is limited effectiveness because of the lack of depth between these two players. A pass made from the 1st Man Offense to the 2nd Man Offense has a greater chance of being intercepted by a covering player. Also, the 2nd Man Offense has little chance of covering the 1st Man Offense if possession is turned over to the opposition. Extensive ground would have to be covered in a limited time. (See Diagram 9-6.)

If the 2nd Man Offense is positioned at the correct distance and at the correct angle but not on the correct side of the 1st Man Offense then his defensive responsibilities cannot be performed in the event the 1st Man Offense loses the ball. This possibility is especially important close to his own goal.

Goalside support requires a position that allows the player to cover the 1st Man Offense on the side closest to the goal. An imaginary line drawn the length of the field from the center of one goal to the center of the other goal divides the field into two. The support player usually positions himself between this line and the 1st Man Offense. (See Diagrams 9-7 and 9-8.)

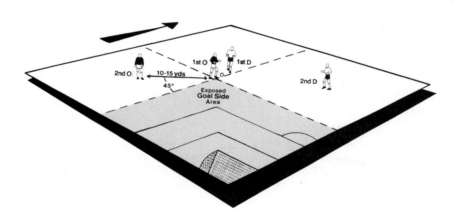

DIAGRAM 9-7

This incorrect positioning of the 2nd Man Offense leaves the goal open to a threat by the 1st Man Defense if he wins the ball. Too much ground and too little time could work against the new defense. A position on the goalside of the 1st Man Offense allows all the functions of the 2nd Man Offense to be applied.

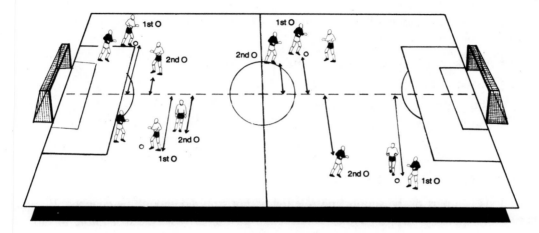

DIAGRAM 9-8

The 2nd Man Offense should position himself closer to the center of the field than the 1st Man Offense. This allows for a sound goalside defensive position should possession be given up. The 2nd Man Offense can also exploit the vital area in the middle of the field much more quickly.

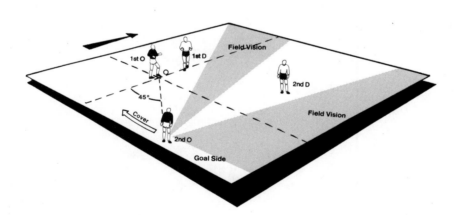

DIAGRAM 9-9

The 2nd Man Offense is now in the correct supporting position of a 45-degree angle on the goal side. This illustration shows the passing possibilities open to him through a wider view of the field as well as his access to the defensive cover area.

The correct angle of 45 degrees on the goal side (illustrated in Diagram 9-9) allows all options to be covered; for example:

- A wide range of passing possibilities is available.
- Vision of the field is enhanced.
- This supporting position is easily seen by the 1st Man Offense.
- The defensive role can be applied quickly if it is required.
- The safety pass to the 2nd Man Offense is assured.

Communication With 1st Man Offense

This is a part of the supporting role that is not stressed enough by coaches. Players do not have to possess all the physical and mental attributes of a Pelé to be able to talk. The information that is given out by the 2nd Man Offense must be short, loud, and to the point. Time does not allow for a verbal dissertation. Words such as "Support" or "Help" will suffice. Some support players prefer to give out more information such as, "If you need me I'm here" or "Give me the ball" or even "I have you covered."

If the message is given quickly and in a loud voice the 1st Man Offense becomes assured that there is assistance if he requires it. This in turn leads to a buildup in confidence for the 1st Man Offense if he attempts to dribble past the defender. Verbal directions during play can pay dividends throughout a game. Players must have confidence in their own ability if they are to instill it in others.

DRILLS

DRILL #1

| PLAYING POSITION: 2ND MAN OFFENSE/SUPPORT |

| COACHING LEVEL: WITHOUT OPPOSITION |

| KEY COACHING POINTS: DISTANCE, ANGLE, & COMMUNICATION |

You should first walk the group through the different aspects of the 2nd Man Offense. Players must first see what is required before they can perform it with understanding.

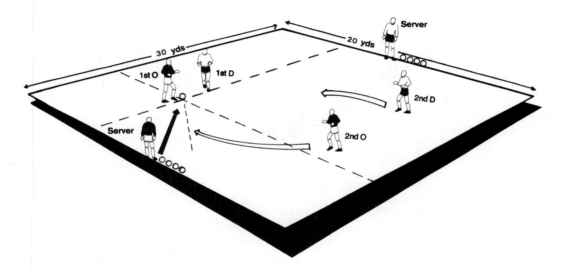

DIAGRAM 9-10

In an area 20 yards x 30 yards two servers are positioned at the ends of the grid, as shown in Diagram 9-10. A 2 vs. 2 situation is then created in this area. After the server has passed the ball into his team, the opportunity arises to present the supporting role of the 2nd Man Offense. The emphasis is placed on:

- Distance
- Angle
- Communication

Defenders will not offer any physical challenge in the form of tackling, neither will they intercept any pass until the group is aware and understands what is involved. As there is no goal to work toward, the support can be given on either side of the 1st Man Offense.

Even though we have stressed that you require a minimum of three offensive players for support, at this stage it is not necessary to include a third player until the drill has progressed to more active forward movement.

DRILL #2

PLAYING POSITION: 2ND MAN OFFENSE/SUPPORT

COACHING LEVEL: PASSIVE OPPOSITION

KEY COACHING POINTS: DISTANCE, ANGLE, & COMMUNICATION

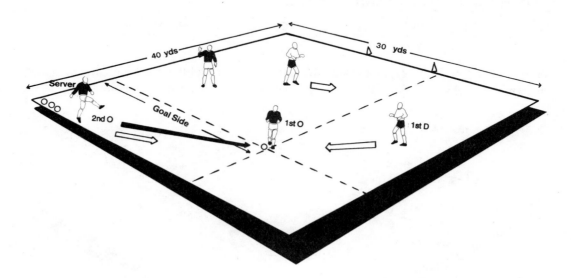

DIAGRAM 9-11

In an area 30 yards x 40 yards a 3 vs. 2 is created with the server acting as an attacker. (See Diagram 9-11.) A goal is set up at one end of the grid. The three attackers move the ball around in an attempt to place it on the goal line between the cones. With the introduction of the goal the 2nd Man Offense must now position himself on the goal side of the 1st Man Offense to cover the defensive situation should it arise.

Emphasis should be placed on having the defense provide passive challenge. The response of the attackers toward the goal and defense is your primary task. The emphasis is placed on the correct support position in terms of:

- Distance
- Angle
- Communication

DRILL #3

PLAYING POSITION: 2ND MAN OFFENSE/SUPPORT

COACHING LEVEL: POSITIVE OPPOSITION

KEY COACHING POINTS: CORRECT FORM
WHEN & WHERE TO SUPPORT

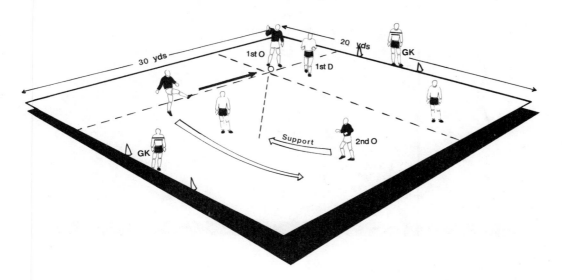

DIAGRAM 9-12

A two-touch condition is imposed on a 3 vs. 3 situation in an area 20 yards x 30 yards. Two goalkeepers are positioned in two goals at either end of the grid. Players must support each other quickly due to the limitation placed on the number of touches. This immediate support provides the opportunity for players to think quickly and respond quickly. The role of the 2nd Man Offense changes rapidly, therefore communication between offensive players is primary. You can also bring up the important consideration of when to support and when not to support.

From a support position the 2nd Man Offense may decide to move wide in an effort to exploit the space on the wing. If this occurs, another attacker must assume the responsibility of the 2nd Man Offense position. The emphasis is placed on:

- Effective communication
- When to and when not to support
- Distance
- Angle

DRILL #4

| PLAYING POSITION: 2ND MAN OFFENSE/SUPPORT |

| COACHING LEVEL: SMALL-SIDED GAME |

| KEY COACHING POINTS: WHEN TO & WHEN NOT TO SUPPORT |

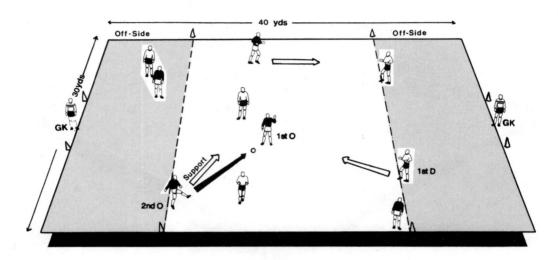

DIAGRAM 9-13

In an area 30 yards x 40 yards a 5 vs. 5 is created. Two goalkeepers are positioned in two goals at either end of the grid. The offside law is applied in the 10-yard area in front of both goals. A two-touch condition can be applied as can a condition requiring short passes along the ground. Unrestricted play can be allowed after a short period. The emphasis is placed on:

- Effective communication
- When to and when not to support
- Distance
- Angle

DRILL #5

| PLAYING POSITION: 2ND MAN OFFENSE/SUPPORT |

| COACHING LEVEL: TEAM TACTICS |

| KEY COACHING POINTS: WHEN TO & WHEN NOT TO SUPPORT |

A team tactic employed with the playing position of 2nd Man Offense will very often involve other players. Coaches strive to combine movements in an effort to confuse the defense. One example of combining movement with a change in direction can be found in the use of the 2nd Man Offense as a pivot player for the attack. This situation can be used in any area of the field.

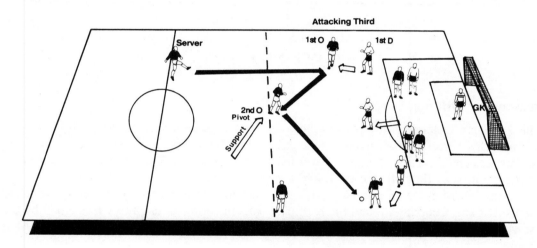

DIAGRAM 9-14

In a half-field area a server passes the ball through and into the attacking third. As soon as an attacker has possession, a support player must be positioned and ready to receive the ball. This 2nd Man Offense must switch play by passing the ball over to the far wing. This move stretches a defense wide before any form of penetration can be effective. This form of pass can be played over a wider distance when it is being brought out of the defensive third. The emphasis is placed on:

- Switching play through the pivot play of the 2nd Man Offense
- When to and when not to support
- Distance
- Angle
- Communication

CHAPTER 10

2nd Man Defense:

Player Supporting the 1st Man Defense

COACHING POINTS

Reasons for Offering Support

The 2nd Man Defense is the player who is directly supporting the 1st Man Defense from behind. This covering position denies the offense any threat directly at goal. There is a range of distances and directions that this player may be positioned in. These positions will depend on the position of the ball, the goal, and threatening attackers.

The 2nd Man Defense must realize that his function is primarily concerned with the events that are occurring around the ball. The outcome of the attempt to win the ball by the 1st Man Defense provides the necessary information for subsequent action by the 2nd Man Defense.

Types of Support

The 2nd Man Defense is responsible to the 1st Man Defense in three ways:

- *Defensive possibilities*. Should the 1st Man Defense be beaten, the 2nd Man Defense can convert his role into that of 1st Man Defense quickly.

- *Attacking possibilities*. Should the 1st Man Defense gain possession, the 2nd Man Defense can convert his role into that of 2nd Man Offense quickly.

- *Mental reassurance*. His reassurance, both verbally and positionally, allows the 1st Man Defense to evaluate the situation with more confidence. This can be observed when the 1st Man Defense goes to make a tackle.

The 2nd Man Defense is limited in any tactical plan by the coach. A single defender is only one part of the whole defense, and his actions contribute toward the overall plan only when combined with the work of others.

There are three factors that should be taught concerning the positioning of the 2nd Man Defense in relation to the 1st Man Defense:

- Distance
- Angle
- Communication

Distance From 1st Man Defense

The distance of this supporting player is determined by where the ball is on the field.

In the defensive third of the field, the support will be closer to the 1st Man Defense (5-10 yards). If this 1st Man Defense is beaten, the 2nd Man Defense must move in quickly before the attacker regains his balance. The play must be destroyed close to goal. Other attacking players are just as dangerous. The 2nd Man Defense must be mentally alert at all times to react to any pass made around the area of the ball.

In the middle third of the field, the 2nd Man Defense works together with the 1st Man Defense to redirect the threat from the 1st Man Offense. This distance is between 10 and 15 yards.

In the attacking third of the field, there is more concern for the space around the ball. No immediate threat can form on goal at this distance. This allows the 2nd Man Defense more space and time to cover the areas through which a pass can be made. This distance is between 10 and 20 yards.

If the 2nd Man Defense is too close to the 1st Man Defense, attackers can play the ball past these two defenders with very little effort. This takes two defenders out of the game instead of only one.

If the 2nd Man Defense is too far away, then the area immediately behind the 1st Man Defense is exposed. There is also the threat of the 2nd Man Offense moving behind the 1st Man Defense, forcing the 2nd Man Defense to make up ground quickly. As with the offensive support, a balance has to be achieved. (See Diagrams 10-1, 10-2, and 10-3.)

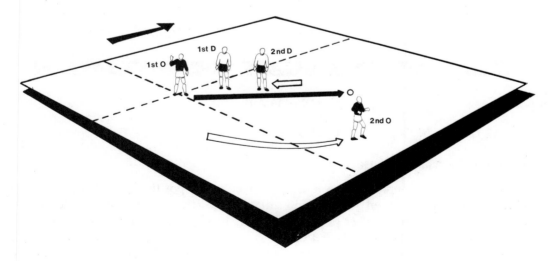

DIAGRAM 10-1
A quick pass can take both defenders out of the game if the 2nd Man Defense moves too close.

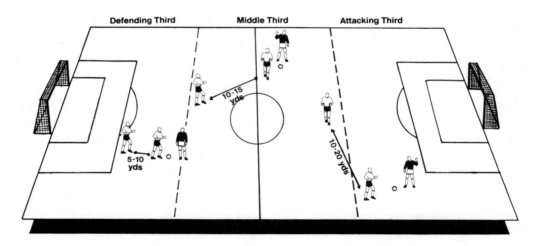

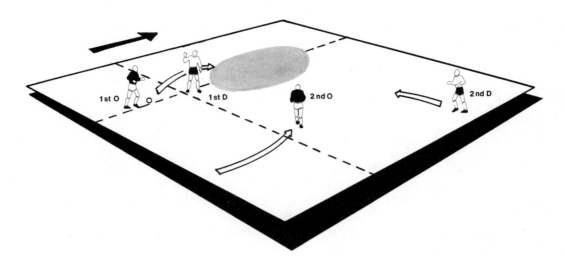

DIAGRAM 10-2
The space behind the 1st Man Defense can be exploited by either a dribble from the 1st Man Offense or a run by the 2nd Man Offense. In this situation, the 2nd Man Defense has too much ground to cover.

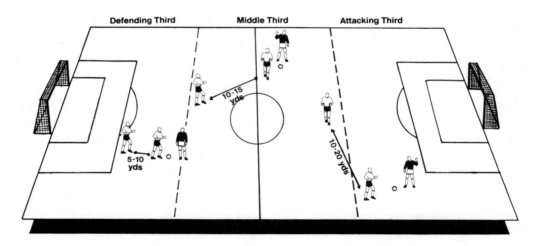

DIAGRAM 10-3
The approximate distance between the 2nd Man Defense and the 1st Man Defense should be different in different areas of the field.

Angle From 1st Man Defense

The angle of the supporting player is determined by the positioning of opponents. This angle must balance the need to offer immediate support to the 1st Man Defense with observing the movements of other players around the ball, especially the 2nd Man Offense. The best supporting angle is usually at 45 degrees from the 1st Man Defense on the goal side.

If the 2nd Man Defense is directly behind the 1st Man Defense there is little advantage in his position because there is limited vision of the field, no realistic effort can be made to intercept the ball, no pressure is placed on the 2nd Man Offense, the direct route to goal is uncovered, and the 1st Man Defense has limited vision of his support.(See Diagram 10-4.)

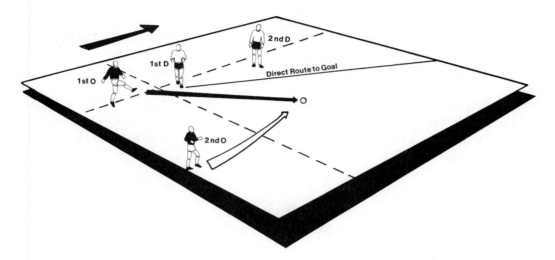

DIAGRAM 10-4
The 2nd Man Defense should not be positioned directly behind the 1st Man
Defense because the direct route to goal is exposed.

If the 2nd Man Defense is positioned directly alongside the 1st Man Defense there is
limited effectiveness because of the lack of depth between these two players. This lack of
depth means that the critical space behind the 1st Man Defense is exposed, a through-pass
will destroy the defensive cover due to the defense being caught "square" or "flat," and if the
1st Man Defense win the ball, he has no support for himself. (See Diagram 10-5.)

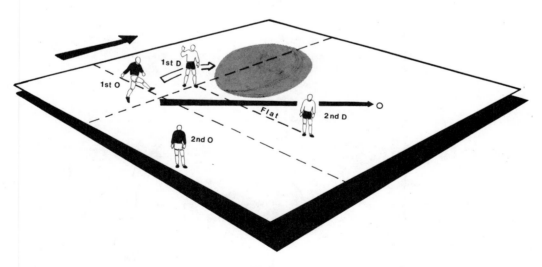

DIAGRAM 10-5
The 2nd Man Defense should not be positioned directly alongside the 1st Man
Defense because the distance to the area behind the 1st Man Defense is too great
while a through-pass can destroy both players' positions.

If the 2nd Man Defense is positioned at the correct distance and at the correct angle but
on the wrong side of the 1st Man Defense then a direct route to goal is exposed to the 1st Man
Offense and to other attacking players making runs into this area.

   The goalside support required is the same as for the offensive support. If the 2nd Man Offense positions himself on the incorrect side of the 1st Man Offense, the 2nd Man Defense should not follow him across, or the critical space and direct route to goal are again exposed. The main responsibility of the 2nd Man Defense is toward directly assisting the 1st Man Defense.

   An offensive support player will sometimes move to the outside with the intention of drawing the 2nd Man Defense away from his position. When this happens the 1st Man Offense is faced with a 1 vs. 1 situation and plenty of space in which to perform his role. (See Diagrams 10-6 and 10-7.)

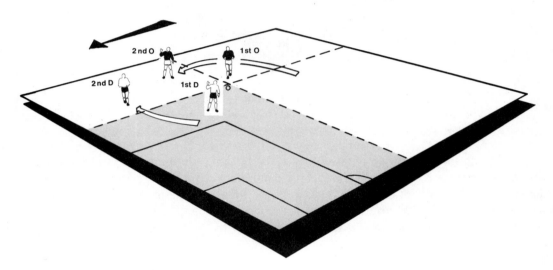

DIAGRAM 10-6
This incorrect positioning of the 2nd Man Defense leaves the goal exposed to the threat from the 1st Man Offense. By moving wide, the 2nd Man Offense has drawn the 2nd Man Defense away from his supporting position.

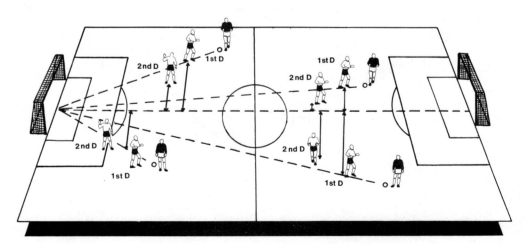

DIAGRAM 10-7
The 2nd Man Defense should position himself closer to the center of the field than the 1st Man Defense in order to cover the direct route to goal.

The correct angle of 45 degrees on the goal side (illustrated in Diagram 10-8) allows all options to be covered; for example:

- The critical space behind the 1st Man Defense can be covered.
- The 2nd Man Offense can be pressured.
- The supporting position is easily seen by the 1st Man Defense.
- The transition to offense can be made that much quicker by the correct offensive support already present.

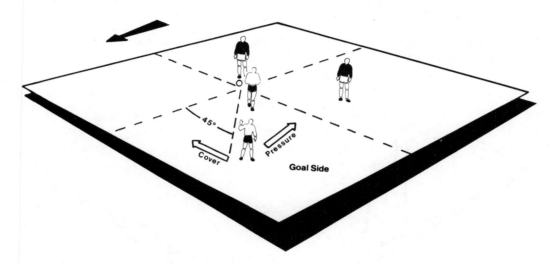

DIAGRAM 10-8

The correct supporting position of the 2nd Man Defense restricts the threat from the attacking team.

Communication With 1st Man Defense

Confusion arises in a defense if players fail to communicate with each other. Informing teammates about immediate or developing situations is vital to the integral working relationship that is sought by players. Commands must be short, loud, and to the point.

Confidence is built and becomes contagious throughout the defense when players begin constructive communication.

DRILLS

DRILL #1

| PLAYING POSITION: 2ND MAN DEFENSE/SUPPORT |

| COACHING LEVEL: WITHOUT OPPOSITION |

| KEY COACHING POINTS: DISTANCE, ANGLE, & COMMUNICATION |

The coach should implement a drill similar to that used in the offensive support to highlight the defensive principles.

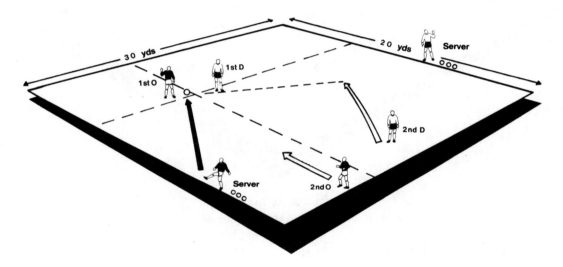

DIAGRAM 10-9

In an area 20 yards x 30 yards two servers are positioned at the ends of the grid. A 2 vs. 2 is set up in this area. After the server has passed the ball into his team the defense must react quickly. You should stress the position of the 2nd Man Defense in relation to the ball and the attackers. Stop the drill at the correct time to emphasize:

- Distance
- Angle
- Communication

As there is no goal at this early stage the 2nd Man Defense concerns himself with all aspects except goalside. He poses no challenge to the offense; rather, moving quickly into a sound defensive support position is sufficient work for the 2nd Man Defense at this stage.

DRILL #2

PLAYING POSITION: 2ND MAN DEFENSE/SUPPORT

COACHING LEVEL: PASSIVE OPPOSITION

KEY COACHING POINTS: DISTANCE, ANGLE, & COMMUNICATION

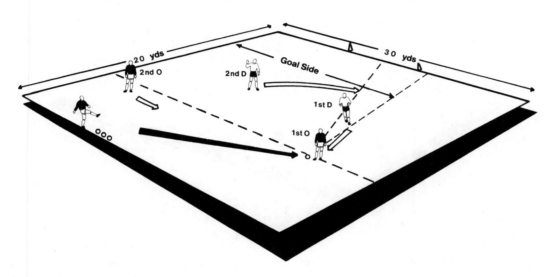

DIAGRAM 10-10

In an area 20 yards × 30 yards, with a goal set up at one end, a ball is served into a 2 vs. 2. The attackers must move the ball onto the goal line between the cones. With the introduction of the goal in this drill, the 2nd Man Defense must now position himself goalside of the 1st Man Defense to cover the direct route to goal. The emphasis is placed on the correct support position in terms of:

- Distance
- Angle
- Communication

DRILL #3

| PLAYING POSITION: 2ND MAN DEFENSE/SUPPORT |

| COACHING LEVEL: POSITIVE OPPOSITION |

| KEY COACHING POINTS: DISTANCE, ANGLE, & COMMUNICATION |

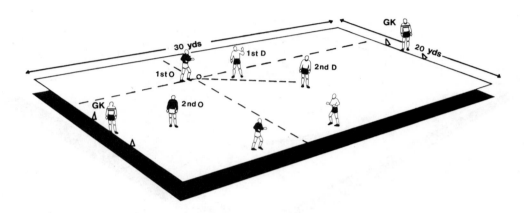

DIAGRAM 10-11

In an area 20 yards x 30 yards two goalkeepers are positioned in goals while a 3 vs. 3 is set up. The correct defensive support must be maintained at all times. Only one defender has to take up this position. The third defender has other responsibilities, which will be discussed later in the book. This role of 2nd Man Defense changes frequently, so allow all three defenders the opportunity to practice it. The emphasis must be placed on:

- The 2nd Man Defense directing his attention toward the ball through the correct distance, angle, and communication

Movement in the form of overlaps by the 2nd Man Offense should be acknowledged by the 2nd Man Defense but not acted upon. If there is a direct threat on goal, other defenders will track down this player and deny him any further advantage.

DRILL #4

PLAYING POSITION: 2ND MAN DEFENSE/SUPPORT

COACHING LEVEL: SMALL-SIDED GAME

KEY COACHING POINTS: DISTANCE, ANGLE, & COMMUNICATION WHEN TO & WHEN NOT TO SUPPORT

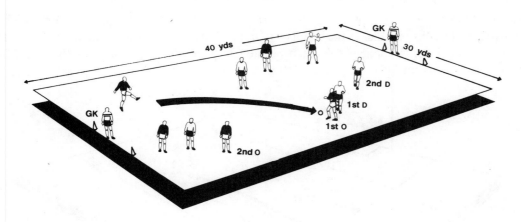

DIAGRAM 10-12

In an area 30 yards x 40 yards a 5 vs. 5 is set up. A goalkeeper is positioned in a goal at each end of the grid. Impose a two-touch condition for a limited time to emphasize the quick defensive support needed in different areas of the field. The function of the 2nd Man Defense now becomes divided among players, as this role is passed over to different players at different times.

The emphasis is placed on:

- The length of time it takes to change defensive roles
- Effective communication
- Distance
- Angle

DRILL #5

| PLAYING POSITION: 2ND MAN DEFENSE/SUPPORT |

| COACHING LEVEL: TEAM TACTICS |

| KEY COACHING POINTS: DISTANCE, ANGLE, & COMMUNICATION |
| WHEN TO & WHEN NOT TO SUPPORT |

The 2nd Man Defense is a player who is part of a total picture. The quality with which a defensive unit works together is the result of individual players performing their specific roles at the correct time. A tactical role incorporated into the defensive unit for the 2nd Man Defense is in directing play across the field.

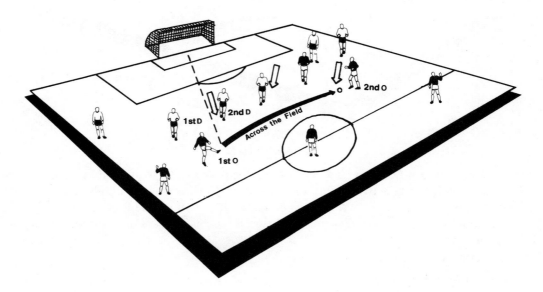

DIAGRAM 10-13

The attacking team begins with the ball at either side of the field at the halfway line. The defense restricts forward movement by applying the offside trap and forcing play across the field. The 2nd Man Defense squeezes up closer than normal as the 1st Man Defense delays slightly further away from the ball than normal. This denies the offense any major forward movement, as other defensive players begin to track down other attackers attempting to move behind the defense. The emphasis is placed on:

- Allowing the 2nd Man Defense to work closely with the 1st Man Defense to initiate the movement of forcing play across the field
- Effective communication

CHAPTER 11

3rd Man Offense: Players Creating and Utilizing Space

COACHING POINTS

In following the ripples out and away from the ball, every other player on offense and defense plays an important role as the team concept now begins to take shape. When reference is made to the 3rd Man on both Offense and Defense, you are concerned with more than one player. You are concerned with the rest of the team, but for simplicity we are referring to them collectively as the 3rd Man.

Difficulties in Coaching This Position

The 3rd Man on both Offense and Defense is the most complex position to teach. The reason for this stems from the fact that you are dealing with a group of players who are not in the immediate area of the ball.

All 3rd Man Offense players are attempting to create space in order to utilize space. In creating space through coordinated team play a player can open up an area to be used by other offensive players; in utilizing space through coordinated team play a player can receive a pass. To achieve both aspects of team play, players must understand the game as a whole.

Offensive players can cause confusion in the defense by making intelligent runs to destroy the balance that a defense aims to achieve. Since modern-day defenses are highly organized, methods of attack must be unlimited.

There are many productive outcomes which can stem from creative play. All should be explored at some point in time. It is only then that the total picture begins to develop and attacking play continues to be unlimited.

Teaching Creativity and Unpredictability

In teaching the 3rd Man Offense it must be understood that space can be created through the combined movements of two or more players.

- If an attacker moves and a defender moves with him, space is created for the 1st Man Offense to utilize.
- If an attacker moves and a defender moves with him, space is created for other players to utilize.
- If an attacker moves and a defender does not move with him, space can be utilized with an immediate pass to this player.

Throughout your teaching of the 3rd Man Offense, emphasize to the players that making a run is only part of the play. The pass that is made from the 1st Man Offense has to be performed and received correctly. It is therefore necessary for all players to play with their heads up in an effort to both make a play and receive a play.

The runs that the 3rd Man Offense undertakes are not predictable, prescribed set moves that have to be made at set times. A player who understands the game as a whole will choose one move over another as he adapts to the situation presented to him by the defense.

Overlap Run

A run that is made from behind the 1st Man Offense and to the outside of this player is referred to as an overlap run. It can be an effective move to either create or utilize space. A player behind the ball can use his view of the field to interpret the development of a play ahead of the ball. With the benefit of this field vision the overlapping player can then react quickly to take advantage of a defensive lapse in concentration. The player making the overlap must:

- Decide at what moment to make his run. This will be determined by the defensive positioning ahead of the ball.
- Increase the pace of his run to move ahead of the ball. He must keep moving forward at this accelerated pace even after a defender has been beaten.
- Communicate with the 1st Man Offense by advising him of when to hold the ball and of when the pass forward would be advantageous to the situation.

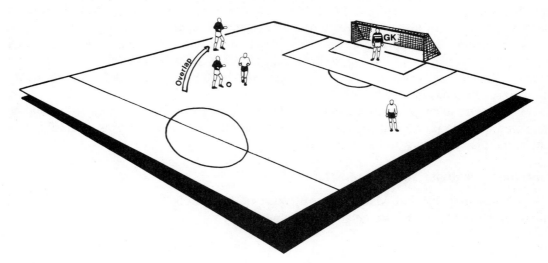

DIAGRAM 11-1
A 2 vs. 1 situation is quickly created against the 1st Man Defense by the overlapping run.

Players can make an overlap run from anywhere on the field. It is usually made out toward the wings to increase the width of the offense. The support player is not the only player who can make this run. Any player can move forward on an overlap as long as the run is made from behind the ball.

An overlap run can utilize space by forcing a 2 vs. 1 situation against the 1st Man Defense. This happens most often when there is little or no defensive support. (See Diagram 11-1.) The player in possession now has the option of passing the ball wide to the player making the overlap run or he can take the defender on in a 1 vs. 1.

An overlap run can create space by removing the defensive support from the area so it can be used by the 1st Man Offense. (See Diagrams 11-2 and 11-3.)

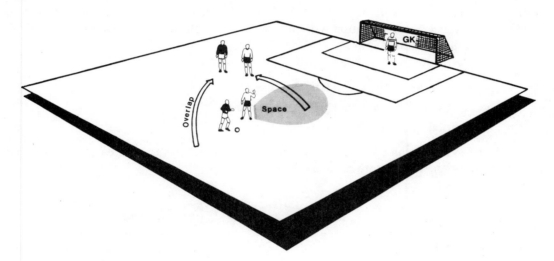

DIAGRAM 11-2

Space has been created behind the 1st Man Defense by the movement of the 2nd Man Defense in going across to cover the attacker.

DIAGRAM 11-3

The 2nd Man Offense does not always make the overlap run. The run can also be made by any player who takes advantage of the situation ahead of the ball.

Blind-side Run

A run that is made behind a defender is referred to as a blind-side run. The term *behind* is used to describe the area between the goal and the defender. A defender cannot acknowledge the run of an attacker if he cannot see him. Defenders are instructed to keep play in front of them while attackers are encouraged to move into positions alongside and behind defenders.

The blind-side run can destroy the covering positions of a defense because defenders are drawn across the field in pursuit of the attacker. The width principle associated with attacking play can be seen in the blind-side run when it is performed from the middle of the field out wide to the wing. Communicating with the 1st Man Offense is done more through the visual presence of the 3rd Man Offense than through the verbal information that is usually given out. A run that is made behind a defender can be seen by the player in possession and therefore any verbal communication will only inform the defender of the whereabouts of the player making the blind-side run.

The angle of this run is dependent upon:

- The positioning of the defenders ahead of the ball
- The positioning of the attackers ahead of the ball
- The position of the ball on the field

A blind-side run can utilize space by moving the attacker into an area of the field that defenders find hard to cover. (See Diagram 11-4.)

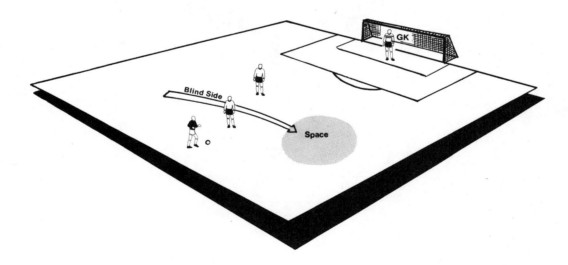

DIAGRAM 11-4
A blind-side run is made by utilizing the space behind the 1st Man Defense. The player in possession can then pass the ball to this attacker.

A blind-side run can create space by forcing the covering defender across the field to open up the area behind the 1st Man Defense. (See Diagrams 11-5 and 11-6.)

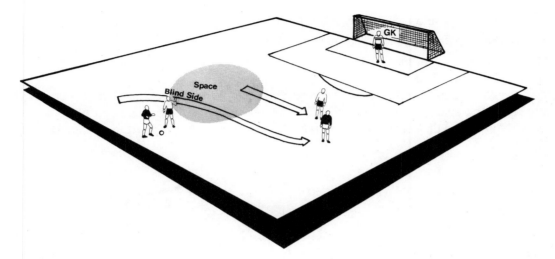

DIAGRAM 11-5
The covering defender is drawn across the field by the blind-side run of the attacker. Space is created behind the 1st Man Defense.

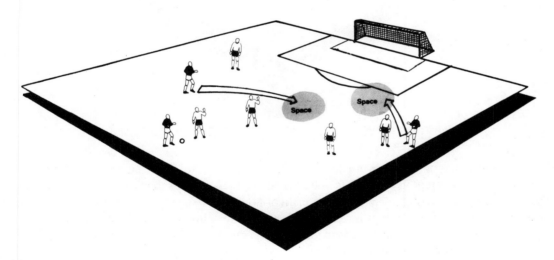

DIAGRAM 11-6
Blind-side runs can be made by any attacking player who attempts to move behind defenders. The offside law can restrict the success rate of these runs the closer they are made to goal.

Diagonal Run

Diagonal runs are usually made in the opponent's half of the field. The offside law often determines whether the run covers a short or long distance. Players who run up and down the field create few problems for defenders. This brand of "channel soccer" becomes predictable and unimaginative. Diagonal runs can be made from:

- The wings into the middle of the field
- The middle of the field out to the wings

The most dangerous of these two runs is the first one because it threatens the critical area in the middle of the field.

When a diagonal run is made from the wings into the middle of the field, it is employed more to utilize space. This inside run allows the player in possession the opportunity to pass the ball through to the penetrating 3rd Man Offense for a shooting opportunity. (See Diagram 11-7.)

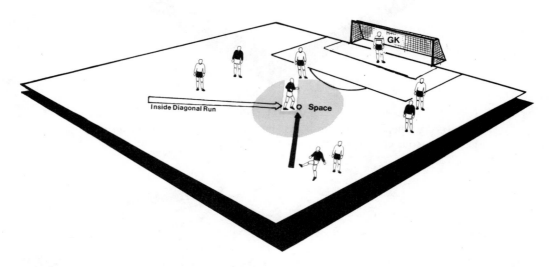

DIAGRAM 11-7
The inside diagonal run is made to utilize space in the vital area of the field.

When a diagonal run is made from the middle of the field out to the wings, it is employed more to create space. This outside run is less dangerous than the inside run because the attackers are moving away from the critical area. This space can also be used by other attacking players if defenders have been drawn away with this diagonal run. A 1 vs. 1 situation can be established if the outside diagonal run removes the 2nd Man Defense from his supporting role. (See Diagram 11-8.)

Diagonal runs are effective in disrupting a zone defense because of the area that is covered by the run across the field and the run up the field. A long diagonal run has the effect of occupying many zones in a shorter time. More defenders become involved with tracking down this player. When performed over a longer distance, this often leads to confusion.

An effective result of diagonal running is seen when more than one player makes a run to open up the middle of the field. This is referred to as a split diagonal run and involves two attacking players moving in opposite directions from the middle of the field to the wings. This is an attempt to create space between central defenders which can then be split by other attacking players moving forward from deep positions. (See Diagram 11-9.)

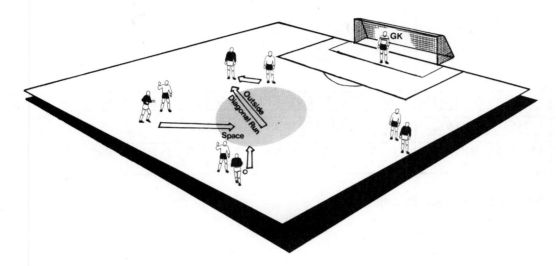

DIAGRAM 11-8

The outside diagonal run creates space in the middle of the field which can be
utilized by the 1st Man Offense or other attacking players.

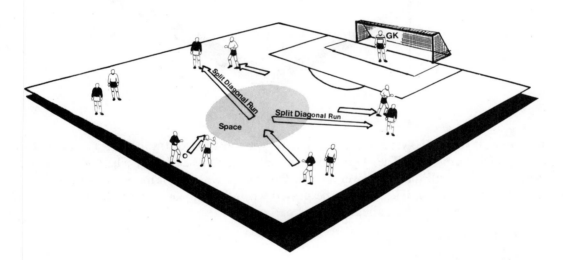

DIAGRAM 11-9

A split diagonal run can create space between central defenders if it is timed
correctly. Other attackers can then utilize this space.

DRILLS

DRILL #1

PLAYING POSITION: 3RD MAN OFFENSE/CREATING & UTILIZING SPACE

COACHING LEVEL: WITHOUT OPPOSITION

KEY COACHING POINTS: THESE WILL VARY DEPENDING UPON THE RUN BEING COACHED

Overlap Run—Walk-through

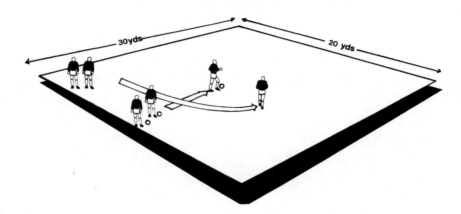

DIAGRAM 11-10

In an area 20 yards x 30 yards two lines of players are positioned 10 yards apart on the line, as shown in Diagram 11-10. The players in the middle of the line each have a ball while the other group of players will make the overlap run. One player with a ball moves forward while his partner makes his run. The ball can be passed when the run has been performed correctly. The emphasis at the walk-through stage is on:

- Effective communication
- Timing of the run
- Speed of the run
- Quality of the pass

Blind-side Run—Walk-through

Two groups are arranged as in the overlap, illustrated in Diagram 11-11. A defender is added as a marker around which the blind-side run is made. The player in possession must release the pass at the most advantageous time to capitalize on the run being made. The emphasis is placed on:

- Correct execution
- Timing the run

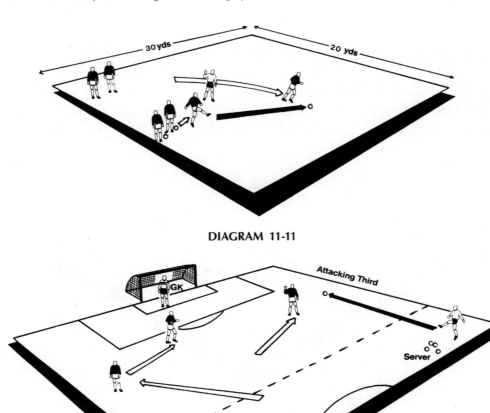

DIAGRAM 11-11

DIAGRAM 11-12

- Speed of the run
- Quality of the pass

Diagonal Run—Walk-through

A small group of players is allowed unrestricted movement in the attacking third of the field. (See Diagram 11-12.) Two servers are positioned close to the halfway line. The attacking players make diagonal runs from the wings to the middle and from the middle to the wings. A ball is then played into one of these players. This very basic drill provides the opportunity for players to work on:

- Changing pace and direction
- Timing their runs
- Understanding the different areas within the attacking third

DRILL #2

PLAYING POSITION: 3RD MAN OFFENSE/CREATING & UTILIZING SPACE

COACHING LEVEL: PASSIVE OPPOSITION

KEY COACHING POINTS: THESE WILL VARY DEPENDING UPON THE RUN BEING COACHED

Overlap Run

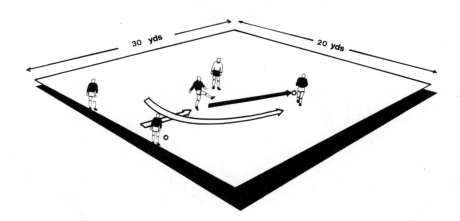

DIAGRAM 11-13

A defender is now placed in the drill who directs his attention to the player in possession. The overlapping player will make his move and receive the pass. (See Diagram 11-13.) Ensure that the pass is played correctly and that the run is timed correctly.

Blind-side Run

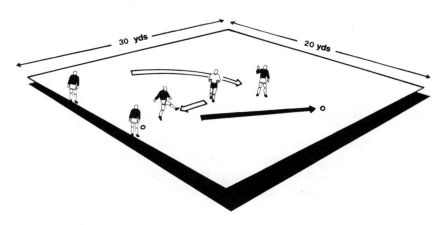

DIAGRAM 11-14

The defensive responsibility of the defender is gradually increased as he approaches and delays the player in possession. (See Diagram 11-14.) The blind-side run and the pass that is played forward must both be timed correctly. Good field vision now begins to play a more important part in the drill as more players are introduced.

Diagonal Run

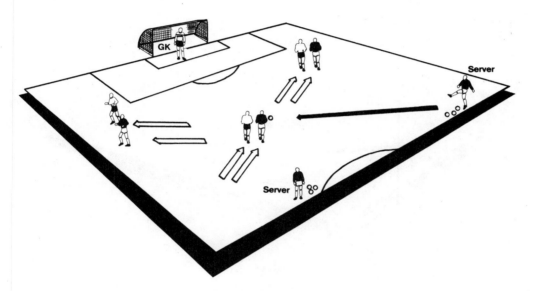

DIAGRAM 11-15

Defenders are now introduced as marking players, as illustrated in Diagram 11-15. They follow the movements of the attackers but offer no physical challenge. You should attempt to create movement that is constructive in both creating and utilizing the space that is available. At this stage a large amount of space has already been created allowing the players an area to work in that does not hinder progress.

DRILL #3

| PLAYING POSITION: 3RD MAN OFFENSE/CREATING & UTILIZING SPACE |

| COACHING LEVEL: POSITIVE OPPOSITION |

| KEY COACHING POINTS: WHEN TO USE ONE MOVE OVER ANOTHER |

Overlap Run

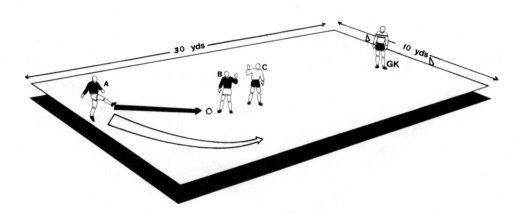

DIAGRAM 11-16

In a more restricted area of 10 yards × 30 yards a 2 vs. 1 is created with a goalkeeper positioned at the end of the grid. (See Diagram 11-16.) Player A passes the ball to player B who must then turn with the ball. As soon as the pass has been released, player A makes an overlapping run. Player B is marked by player C. The decision now has to be made whether to play the ball forward for this overlapping player or whether to challenge the defender with a dribble. This final decision is dependent upon the movement of player C:

- If player C is unbalanced, then the pass should be made to the overlapping player A.
- If player C moves toward the overlapping player A, then player B should advance the ball or take the shot.

The emphasis is placed on:

- A quick turn by player B once he has possession
- A well-timed run by player A
- Communication between attackers
- The correct decision making by players A and B

Blind-side Run

In an area 10 yards x 30 yards a 2 vs. 1 is created with a goalkeeper positioned at the

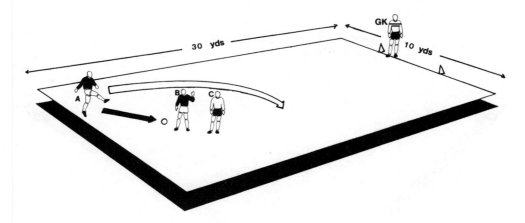

DIAGRAM 11-17

end of the grid. (See Diagram 11-17.) Player A passes the ball to player B who then turns with the ball and faces the defender, player C. Player A makes his move to get behind the defender. Player B must then decide whether to pass the ball to player A or whether to dribble past player C.

The choice is determined by:

- The reaction of player C to the blind-side run
- The quality of the blind-side run

Other factors:

- If player C is unbalanced then the pass should be made to player A.
- If player C turns to deny the blind-side run of player A then player B should advance the ball or take the shot.

The emphasis is placed on:

- A quick turn by player B once he has possession
- A well-timed run by player A
- The correct decision making of players A and B

There is little benefit to be derived from the blind-side run if the player making it talks continually. The defender is then able to locate the run much easier than if a call was made at the last moment.

Diagonal Runs

The defenders are now unrestricted in their movements. The attackers must move to create space and then utilize space through runs made from deeper positions close to the halfway line. (See Diagram 11-18.) The server must release the ball at the moment that is most advantageous to the player making the run.

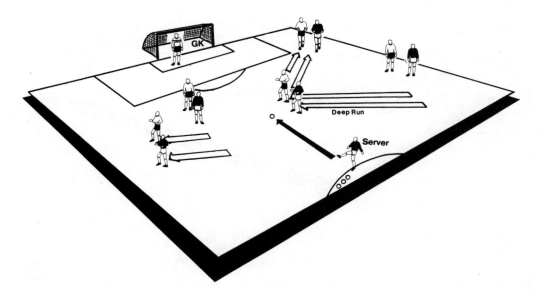

DIAGRAM 11-18

The emphasis is placed on:

- Certain players creating space through their runs
- Certain players utilizing this space through their runs

DRILL #4

| PLAYING POSITION: 3RD MAN OFFENSE/CREATING & UTILIZING SPACE |

| COACHING LEVEL: SMALL-SIDED GAME |

| KEY COACHING POINTS: WHEN & WHERE TO CREATE & USE SPACE |

Overlap Run

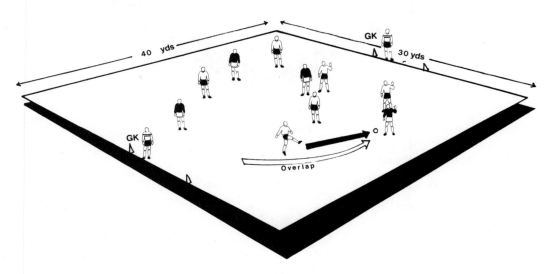

DIAGRAM 11-19

As illustrated in Diagram 11-19, a 5 vs. 5 is set up in an area 30 yards x 40 yards. Inventive play off the ball is encouraged. A player who makes an overlap run and receives the ball while performing it, is awarded a point for his team. Two points are awarded for a goal. In the initial stages, condition the player that after every pass he moves on an overlap run. This must only be practiced briefly as players must be given the opportunity to think more about their responsibilities.

The emphasis is placed on:

• Deciding when to and when not to make the overlap run

• Vision of the field

• Communication

• Thinking ahead

• Timing

Blind-side Run

In the same organizational setup as for the overlap run, the blind-side run is awarded one point for the team successfully completing the movement. (See Diagram 11-20.)

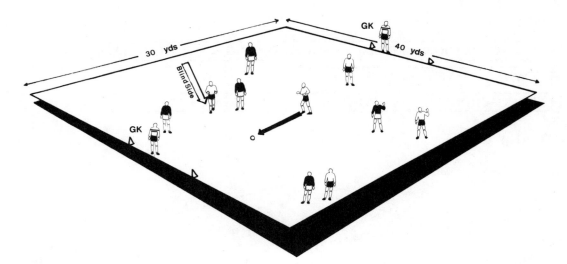

DIAGRAM 11-20

The emphasis is placed on:

- Deciding when to and when not to make the blind-side run
- Vision of the field
- Thinking ahead
- Timing

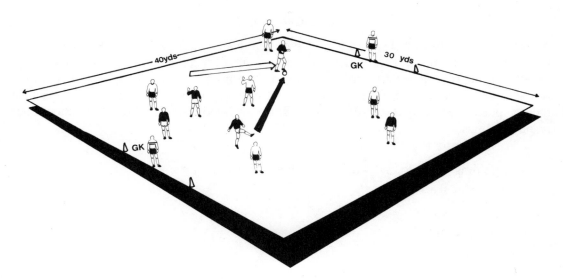

DIAGRAM 11-21

Diagonal Run

A point is awarded for a successful diagonal run. Encourage players to move from deep positions in an attempt to disrupt more than one defender. (See Diagram 11-21.) The emphasis is placed on:

- Deciding when to and when not to make a diagonal run
- Vision of the field
- Communication
- Thinking ahead
- Timing

Players should be encouraged to look for both inside and outside diagonal runs.

DRILL #5

| PLAYING POSITION: 3RD MAN OFFENSE/CREATING & UTILIZING SPACE |

| COACHING LEVEL: TEAM TACTICS |

| KEY COACHING POINTS: WHEN & WHERE TO CREATE & USE SPACE |

The 3rd Man Offense moves in an effort to stretch a defense from end to end and from side to side. If this can be achieved, more space can be utilized and more time is available within which to perform.

The 3rd Man Offense must concentrate on his next move and react quickly when the situation presents itself. Quick execution is paramount to the disruption of a defense, especially in the attacking third of the field. One-touch and two-touch soccer can reap many benefits as a team takes advantage of the situation.

Some coaches frown upon including one-touch soccer in their training sessions. They believe that it is unrealistic to the game of soccer. Unfortunately, it is unrealistic to them only because they have never experienced the benefits that can be gained from it during a game—and that because they have probably never practiced it. Other coaches avoid this style of play because of the demands it makes on the movement of the 3rd Man Offense. In the attacking third of the field there is nothing more pleasing to the eye than a series of well-executed, first-time passes with a finished shot on goal. A defense finds it extremely difficult to defend against this rapid exchange of passes, as their organization loses its effectiveness almost immediately. This is evident when the 1st Man Defense is observed.

The point of attack changes quickly with one-touch soccer and so does the responsibility of this 1st Man Defense. For one-touch play to be productive, the emphasis is mutually shared between the player moving for the ball—3rd Man Offense—and the player passing the ball—1st Man Offense. It is the combined effort of these players that dictates the effectiveness of the outcome.

In working at the Team Tactics level of the 3rd Man Offense, you should direct attention to the different thirds of the field. It is within these areas that attackers must choose on the side of safety or risk.

The involvement of many players in the 3rd Man Offense position means many decisions have to be made. The most frequent choice that is made concerns choosing one form of offensive movement over another. The choice will be based on the structure and positioning of the defense, and the area of the field where the ball is located. Once an offense has an understanding of their task, they can begin to implement their ideas.

The runs that have previously been discussed should be attempted from different areas of the field and through different angles. The attacking players involved in these attacking runs should:

- Attempt to take players from good defensive positions into bad defensive positions
- Attempt to get the ball
- Attempt to keep the ball in view at all times
- Attempt to have as wide a view of the field as possible

The player in possession should:

• Attempt to choose the correct pass and play it to the player in the best position from which to penetrate

The space that is required for effective attacking play must first be created and then utilized. In utilizing space the attacker must move quickly, whether unmarked or incorrectly marked. The outcome of all attacking play should result in a shot on goal.

The individual skills and combined movements must now be coached in the team setting. Different phases of the game require different approaches.

Defensive Third

A team that brings the ball out from their own goal usually finds that space has already been created because of the lack of immediate pressure from the opposition. A team that is applying a full-field, man-to-man marking system forces the offense to create space in all three areas of the field. Once the goalkeeper has possession of the ball his first choice is also the most dangerous in terms of giving up possession. Playing the ball down the middle is the most direct route to goal. The two wing fullbacks will move wide in an attempt to create space by opening up the middle of the field and utilize space by receiving the pass.

The sweeper is an easy outlet pass for the goalkeeper because:

• He has a wide view of the field from this central position.

• It is unlikely that he will be marked.

• He is usually composed.

The offense is now spread from side to side in an attempt to create and utilize the space through the middle of the field. (See Diagram 11-22.)

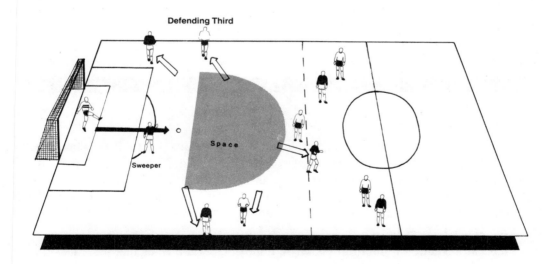

DIAGRAM 11-22

Midfield

A team must control this area of the field to be successful in moving forward and building soundly. The offense must be patient in this build-up phase in order to allow constructive runs to be made ahead of the ball.

An attacking team must experience all-around support in the midfield area. Overlapping is a frequent link play from the middle third into the attacking third. An inventive style of play is to allow the wing fullbacks to move forward on the wings enabling:

- A quick lead pass out to this player
- Defenders to be drawn out to this offensive threat therefore leaving space to be utilized in the middle.

A combination of effective runs off the ball can be attempted from deep positions forward into the attacking third. Diagonal runs play a major part in disrupting both man-to-man and zone defenses, due to the stretching-out that takes place once a run is made in front of the defense. (See Diagram 11-23.) If you decide to work on crossover plays in the middle third, you can condition a man-to-man marking system.

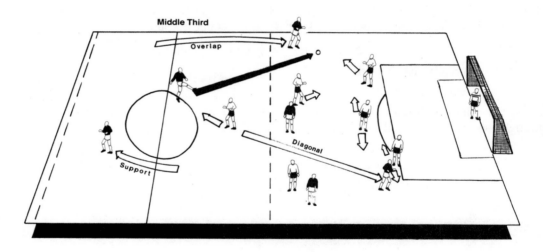

DIAGRAM 11-23

Passes can also be made from the middle third into the attacking third to players getting behind the defense. Both long and short passes can be played into this area from deep positions. The blind-side run is very similar to the diagonal run. The major difference is that a blind-side run has little depth to it. It is usually a "flat" or "square" run made across the field that provides an outlet pass directly behind and to the side of the defender. (See Diagram 11-24.)

You can condition a build-up phase by imposing certain rules that the attackers must adhere to. To expose the 3rd Man Offense impose the condition that every third touch on the ball must be a through-pass into the attacking third. This forces the 3rd Man Offense to think ahead of the immediate situation.

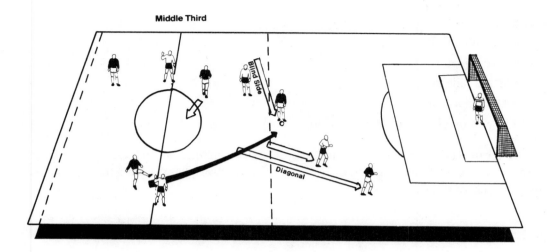

DIAGRAM 11-24

Attacking Third

This is the area of the field where players can exhibit individual flair in tight situations. Movements must be quick and accurate in order to produce results.

One-touch soccer can provide many avenues for success if you are prepared to practice it with your team. The combined movements of attacking players can destroy defensive coverage in this third of the field, due to the pressure placed on the defense to track down players in a limited space.

A server plays the ball into the attacking team who are marked by defenders. (See Diagram 11-25.) Individual and combined skills are necessary in preparing for a shot on goal. The game can be conditioned for:

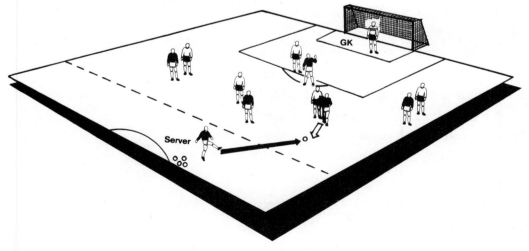

DIAGRAM 11-25

- One-touch play
- Two-touch play
- Overlap run
- Blind-side run
- Diagonal run
- Player moving into defender before checking back for the ball

After the condition has been lifted, players must then think for themselves and make the correct choices at the correct time. Inventive and creative play on the side of risk should always be encouraged.

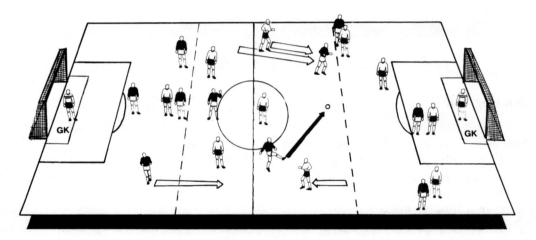

DIAGRAM 11-26

On a full field, inventive and creative play is encouraged in the middle and attacking thirds. (See Diagram 11-26.) The defensive third must contain safety plays that aim to maintain possession. The 3rd Man Offense must:

- Create space through combined movements
- Utilize space through combined movements
- Attack the covering assignments of the defense through combined movements
- Move behind defenders through combined movements

The player with the ball must be prepared to:

- Take risks
- Be inventive
- Be creative
- Look for the shot
- Look for the pass
- Look to dribble

A defense is usually structured to direct any attacking movement out to the wings. The availability of working space provides an offense time in which to build an attack. A ball that is played in toward the middle from the wings poses a major threat because defenders must divide their attention between the wings and the middle.

Crosses

Crosses can be played to three main areas: near post, far post, and middle of the goal.

The 1st Man Offense should play the ball across from the wing only when there is knowledge of the defensive positioning, offensive positioning, and area available.

The 3rd Man Offense must concern himself with the:

- Angle of the run
- Timing of the run
- Finished shot on goal

Angle of the Run

A player attacks the ball by moving into the line of flight, rather than attempting to move across it. If the angle is correct, timing the run can be achieved that much easier. Due to the precise timing needed in striking the ball, it is more difficult for sound contact to be made on the ball when a run is made across the path of the ball. Movement into the ball helps immensely in providing the player with more chance of success.

Timing the Run

The run should be made late, but at a fast pace. Defenders will be able to reorganize their marking assignments quickly if an attacker has moved too early and has to wait for the ball to arrive. The player who meets the ball first has the advantage of playing the ball with limited pressure from the opposition.

Finishing

As with any build-up tactic, the aim is to score a goal. Players must therefore concentrate on making sound contact on the ball. A shot on goal is simply a change in the direction of the ball.

Too many players have a mental block and swing too quickly at the ball. An easy swing or smooth header must accompany the correct angle and timing of the run. Keeping the ball low can be achieved by striking through the upper half.

The 3rd Man Offense must again make decisions. Should he:

- Utilize space by attacking the ball
- Create space by taking defenders away

In all aspects of the 3rd Man Offense, you should ensure that players not only make decisions, but also understand *why* they are making these decisions. It is through this difficult phase of the game that players begin to understand the game as a whole. Soccer is an easy game to learn but a difficult one to master.

CHAPTER 12

3rd Man Defense: Players Denying Space

COACHING POINTS

With the 1st and 2nd Man Defense occupied controlling the immediate point of attack, the remaining 3rd Man Defense has to accept the responsibility of denying space. It is an accepted fact that the main purpose of attacking play is to get behind the defense in order to create scoring opportunities. A defense must oppose this by sealing off the vital spaces and tracking down attacking players. The play will then be kept in front of the defense, denying any form of penetration into the space behind defenders. The 3rd Man Defense aims to prevent any forward penetration either by the ball or by additional attacking players.

It has become more apparent at the youth level that coaches are overly concerned with systems of play, man-to-man marking, and zone defense. The defensive issues of man-to-man and zone are sometimes exaggerated. Playing one style of defense over another is not the solution to all attacking plays. Players should not be built into a style of defense, but instead, a style of defense should be built around the players' individual and group strengths. A team that is physically fit may benefit from a man-to-man defense for part of the game. Players who have excellent field vision and can react quickly to developing situations may derive more benefit from a zone defense.

The important points to remember are:

- Defense is a mixture of marking players and covering space at the same time.
- The closer an attacking team advances toward goal the more concerned the defense is with marking players.
- The further an attacking team is from goal the more concerned the defense is with covering space.

One of the most critical moments in a soccer game occurs when the ball is given back to the opposition. From a defensive standpoint players must react quickly and recover quickly.

A team that has been pushing forward and then loses possession, usually has players ahead of the ball. These players must react and recover in an attempt to keep play in front of them. Failure to recover will lead to a numerical advantage for the offense.

While the 1st and 2nd Man Defense are responsible for closing down the point of attack, the 3rd Man Defense has to assess the situation.

Sealing off the Vital Space—Recovering

Players need to move quickly on the shortest route to protect the area in front of goal. (See Diagram 12-1.) Provided that the 1st Man Defense is in position, recovering players should occupy the support position of the 2nd Man Defense and the marking and covering of the 3rd Man Defense. The recovering players must not retreat too far beyond the 1st Man Defense. They must have a view of the field and an understanding of their role.

- Players recovering on the right side of the field will follow a line toward the right-hand goal post—near post.

- Players recovering in the middle of the field will follow a line toward the middle of the goal.

- Players recovering on the left side of the field will follow a line toward the left-hand goal post—near post.

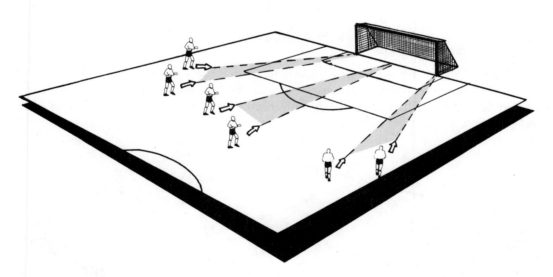

DIAGRAM 12-1
New defenders retreat along imaginary recovery lines following loss of possession.

Once the defenders have taken the correct and shortest recovery route they must concentrate on and perform their defensive responsibilities. Failure to do this can permit further penetration by the ball or other attacking players.

The positioning of the 3rd Man Defense is dependent upon three factors:

- The positions of the attackers

- The position of the goal
- The position of the ball

The 3rd Man Defense can be introduced through a simple reconstruction of a 3 vs 3. This walk-through method is the most productive in terms of putting the concept across.

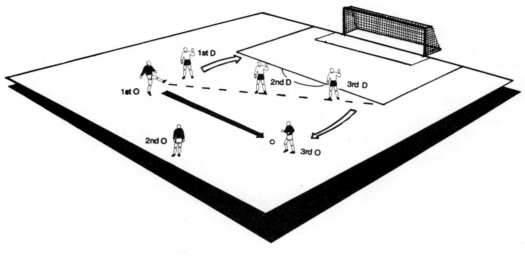

DIAGRAM 12-2

Three attackers are positioned against three defenders. (See Diagram 12-2.) Each player is performing a positional function. Once the ball is passed from the 1st Man Offense across to the 3rd Man Offense the defense must reorganize according to the positions of the attackers, the goal, and the ball.

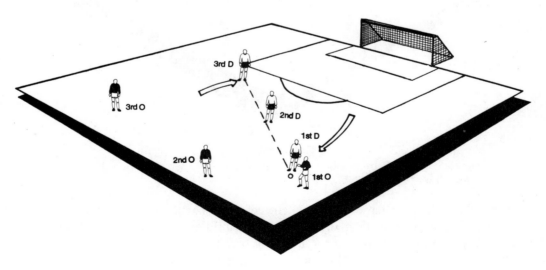

DIAGRAM 12-3

The 2nd Man Defense is used as a pivot player around which the other two defenders revolve. (See Diagram 12-3.) The 3rd Man Defense moves back toward his goal to balance the possible threat against the other two defenders. The 3rd Man Offense is the furthest from the ball and therefore does not pose any immediate threat to the defense. This allows the 3rd Man Defense to cover the 1st and 2nd Man Defense as they attempt to win the ball. There is sufficient time for this 3rd Man Defense to close down his opponent, the 3rd Man Offense, should he receive a pass. The distance that the ball has to travel gives him time to adjust quickly.

If the 2nd Man Offense receives the ball, the defense must again reorganize. The defender who closes down this attacker is usually the defender closest to the ball and on a sound defending angle. In the example given, the 2nd Man Defense moves quickly to delay this attacker. The remaining defenders then balance both sides of the 1st Man Defense as the ball is now in the middle of the field. (See Diagram 12-4.) Both of these defenders function as 2nd Man Defense until the outcome of the 1 vs. 1 around the ball is determined.

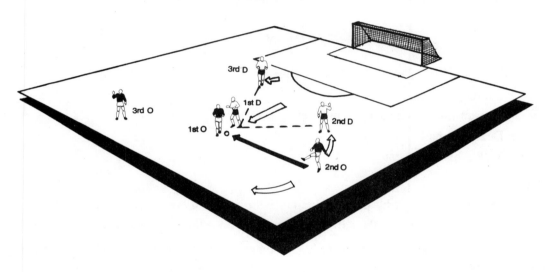

DIAGRAM 12-4

In sealing off the vital spaces, a defense that has recovered can form a defensive zone against the opposition. A zone defense is a series of territorial areas which each individual defender must cover. If an attacker moves into a defender's personal zone, he is covered by this defender until he moves into a different zone. The defensive responsibility is then passed on to another defender. There must be effective communication in all areas of a zone defense, especially from the sweeper and the goalkeeper. The sweeper will deny potential threats on goal by covering all the defenders in front of him. He will slide around the back of the defense on a line drawn from the ball to the middle of the goal. The goalkeeper has to direct the defensive traffic as well as position himself to deal with the direct shot on goal.

Once a defender has taken up the most productive position, he must be aware of balls played into the space behind him and balls played into the feet of his immediate opponent. (See Diagram 12-5.)

DIAGRAM 12-5

Once the ball is played, a defender must attempt to:

- Intercept the pass
- Prevent his opponent from turning
- Delay the ball
- Tackle his opponent

A defense must:

- Destroy the attack by playing the ball with height, distance, and width
- Regain possession of the ball if at all possible once the dangerous play has been made

Once the vital space has been sealed off there is still the threat of attacking runs being made into these spaces. Defenders have to be capable of tracking players and marking them.

Tracking and Marking Players

It was mentioned previously that attacking players must be marked the closer they come to the goal. Unfortunately, ball watching is a frequent mistake made by some defenders, and this tendency to track the ball rather than the player can prove costly in the defending third of the field. The moment that attacking players begin to make their moves, defenders should take this as the cue to respond. It must again be stressed that there are only two reasons for attackers to make runs. They are to create space and utilize space.

Defenders have to determine quickly what type of run is being made and for what purpose. The most dangerous runs are the ones from the wings into the middle. These runs are aimed at utilizing space. When tracking down such a run a defender should, as shown in Diagram 12-6:

- Remain on the goal side of the attacker
- Keep his opponent and the ball in view
- Have an awareness of the position of the goal

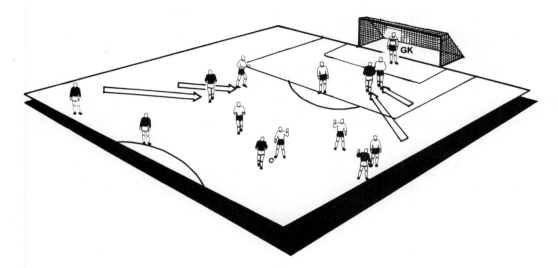

DIAGRAM 12-6
The 3rd Man Defense responds to the diagonal blind-side run of the attacker from the wing into the middle.

One of the least dangerous direct runs is from the middle out to the wings. These runs are aimed at creating space.

Balance in Defense

Defenders have to be prepared to track players, but only for a certain distance. A defender who is drawn all the way out to the wing has opened up the central area of the field. This area can then be quickly exploited by other attacking runs. Defenders must balance their runs between moving away too far and not moving at all. (See Diagram 12-7.)

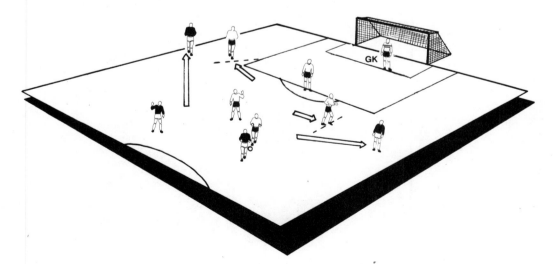

DIAGRAM 12-7
A balanced run by the 3rd Man Defense reduces the chances of offensive pressure from many different directions.

A defender who can successfully balance both options has the opportunity to:

- Intercept a pass made to the wing
- Close down the attacker in time
- Contain the central area of the field

The following drills need to be set up with a restricted offense. In the early stages you can stage an attack by defining certain attacking movements. A defense can then be taught the correct procedure for dealing with these.

Unrestricted offensive play can then be introduced to provide an opportunity for the defense to make their own decisions based upon the situation they find themselves in.

DRILLS

DRILL #1

| PLAYING POSITION: 3RD MAN DEFENSE/DENYING SPACE |

| COACHING LEVEL: WITHOUT OPPOSITION |

| KEY COACHING POINTS: MARKING PLAYERS & COVERING SPACE |

The basic concept of the 3rd Man Defense is explained by the walk-through procedure.

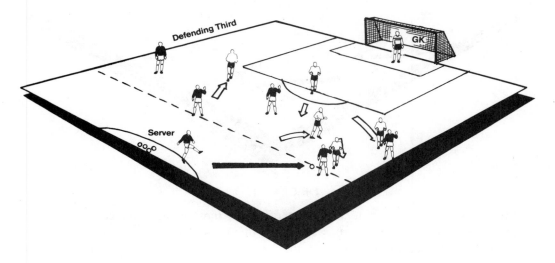

DIAGRAM 12-8

The attacking team is positioned around the attacking third of the field and not allowed to move. The ball is then played to the feet of an attacker. In the initial stages, until the defense has become organized, the ball must be kept stationary when it is controlled. Once the defense is correctly positioned the ball continues on to another player.

The drill should not be rushed as the emphasis is placed on:

• Defenders taking up the correct positions

• Defenders understanding their positions

You may frequently have to stop the play at this level as you attempt to put across the major points that:

• Defenders must react quickly.

• Defenders must maintain vision of both attackers and the ball.

• Defenders must be aware of the position of the goal.

DRILL #2

PLAYING POSITION: 3RD MAN DEFENSE/DENYING SPACE

COACHING LEVEL: PASSIVE OPPOSITION

KEY COACHING POINTS: MARKING PLAYERS & COVERING SPACE

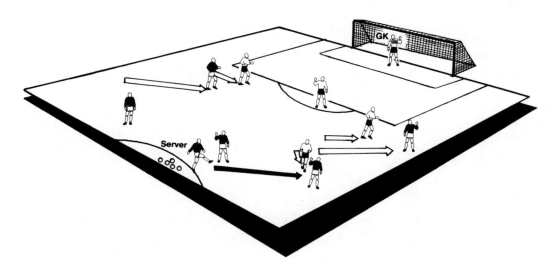

DIAGRAM 12-9

Attacking players now begin to construct offensive movements. You can condition the attackers to attempt only certain runs at a time; this allows you to gradually introduce the defense to their responsibilities against attackers who are now moving. The emphasis is placed on:

- Sealing off the vital space
- Tracking and marking players
- Keeping the play in front of the defense

DRILL #3

| PLAYING POSITION: 3RD MAN DEFENSE/DENYING SPACE |

| COACHING LEVEL: POSITIVE OPPOSITION |

| KEY COACHING POINTS: MARKING PLAYERS & COVERING SPACE |

Recovery runs are now introduced.

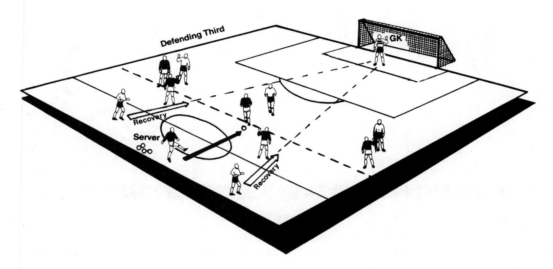

DIAGRAM 12-10

A 5 vs. 5 situation is set up with a goalkeeper. From a position beyond the halfway line a server plays the ball into an attacker. At this point the defense is outnumbered, 5 to 3. Two additional defenders make recovery runs toward their own goal with the intention of:

- Moving along the correct recovery angle
- Moving along the shortest recovery route
- Not recovering too far ahead of the ball
- Concentrating on their responsibilities once they have recovered
- Sealing off vital spaces
- Tracking and marking players who move closer toward goal

DRILL #4

PLAYING POSITION: 3RD MAN DEFENSE/DENYING SPACE

COACHING LEVEL: SMALL-SIDED GAME

KEY COACHING POINTS: MARKING PLAYERS & COVERING SPACE

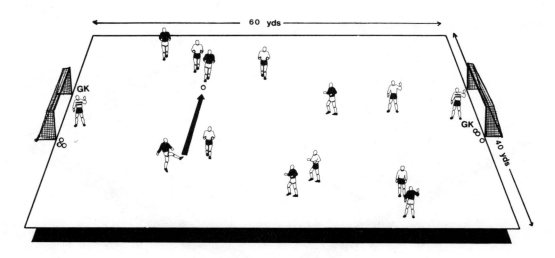

DIAGRAM 12-11

In an area 60 yards x 40 yards a 6 vs. 6 is created with an additional goalkeeper in each goal. Unrestricted play is permitted to allow defenders to react to the many different situations that now confront them. The goalkeeper keeps the game moving by using a supply of balls when the initial ball goes out of play.

The emphasis is placed on:

- Correct decision making

DRILL #5

PLAYING POSITION: 3RD MAN DEFENSE/DENYING SPACE

COACHING LEVEL: TEAM TACTICS

KEY COACHING POINTS: MARKING PLAYERS & COVERING SPACE

Low-Pressure Zone Defense

A defense should respond to attacks in different areas of the field in different ways. No single defensive team tactic can be employed for the total game as the opposition eventually becomes wise to the approach and adapts accordingly.

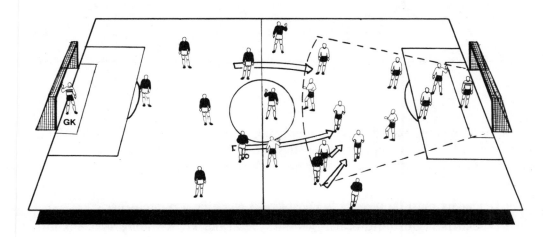

DIAGRAM 12-12

A low-pressure zone defense, as illustrated in Diagram 12-12, permits the defense to:

- Restrict the time and space in the vital area
- Frustrate the offense in the vital area
- Restrict the threatening runs into the middle of the field

All ten players must recover as a team for the tactic to be effective. If only a few players recover, space is made available for the attackers especially in the midfield, the build-up area of the game.

The two main advantages of the zone defense are:

- Economy of movement—chasing becomes less frequent.
- Hiding—a defender's lack of speed can be minimized.

The two main disadvantages of the zone defense are that:

- Mistakes become delegated.
- Concentration can lapse due to defenders not being directly responsible for attackers.

High-Pressure, Man-to-Man Defense in the Defending Third

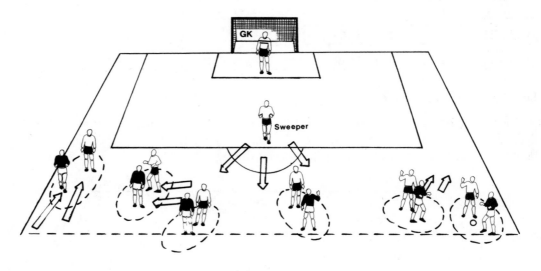

DIAGRAM 12-13

A strict man-to-man defense is employed in the defending third of the field. (See Diagram 12-13.) The sweeper remains free to support the defense from any direction. Outside of this area defenders are concerned with covering space. Two important considerations are:

- Defenders must be physically capable of sustaining a rigorous pace.
- Defenders in this third of the field must react quickly when possession is lost.

CHAPTER 13

Goalkeeping: The Specialist Position

COACHING POINTS

The rules of soccer permit a goalkeeper to use his hands. It is this advantage which separates him from the rest of the team. No single individual can have as much influence on the outcome of a game as can the goalkeeper. He is the one who can shoulder both victory and defeat by his own individual performance. There are three main areas of concern when teaching the skill of goalkeeping:

- Stopping shots
- Positioning
- Distribution

The Ready Position

Basic Stance

A goalkeeper must prepare himself in order to react to a situation that develops. The correct positioning of the body will assist him in this task. The body part that coaches probably neglect the most is the head. Through all aspects of goalkeeper training the head must remain steady while the eyes watch the ball for as long as possible. [See Photo 13-1.]

Hands

The hands should be held at waist height, palms face forward with the fingers spread. The hands should not be held above waist height because one of the most difficult balls to save is the one that is played close to the ground. Keeping the hands low reduces the distance between the ground and the hands.

Feet

The feet are placed shoulder width apart with the body weight forward on the balls of the feet. The legs are slightly bent to allow a "ready" position for springing up or across the goal or to get the body weight down quickly to stop the shot placed low around the ankles.

PHOTO 13-1
GOALKEEPING TECHNIQUE: THE READY POSITION

Stopping Shots—Into the Body: On the Ground

A ball that is played along the ground can be difficult to pick up because of the uneven ground found in many goal areas. It is therefore important for the goalkeeper to place his body directly behind the ball as quickly as possible.

Two forms of collecting the ball are the Long Barrier Technique and the Scoop Technique.

The Long Barrier

The main advantage of collecting the ball in this manner is that it allows vision of the immediate area around the goalkeeper; intruding attackers are quickly observed. It is also a technique the goalkeeper can perform smoothly, with little interruption in the flow of collecting and distributing the ball. [See Photo Series 13-2(A).]

Hands

The hands are held at waist height, palms face forward with the fingers spread. As the ball approaches they are placed out in front of the body on the ground; as the ball touches them, they cushion it up into the chest.

Feet

The feet are positioned sideways to the approaching ball. One knee is placed on the ground sideways, with the lower leg positioned across the path of the ball to prevent it from squeezing through. This long barrier offers a large surface area to face the ball.

PHOTO SERIES 13-2
GOALKEEPING TECHNIQUE: STOPPING SHOTS

INTO THE BODY

(A)
The Long Barrier

(B)
The Scoop

(C
Cupping the Ball
Into the Body

The Scoop Technique

This form of collecting the ball is normally used when the goalkeeper has sufficient time in which to move his body into the line of the ball unchallenged from the opposition. It is more productive when used on a slow shot or backpass. [See Photo Series 13-2(B).]

Hands

The hands are placed behind the ball on the ground. As the ball touches them, they scoop it up into the chest.

PHOTO SERIES 13-2
GOALKEEPING TECHNIQUE: STOPPING SHOTS
(Cont'd)

ABOVE THE BODY

**(D)
The "W" Hand
Position**

**(E)
Taking the Ball
in the Air**

Feet

The feet are raised up on the toes and positioned close together. The legs are bent slightly at the knees.

Stopping Shots—Into the Body: Waist and Chest Height

As balls are played off the ground and into the goalkeeper's body only a slight adjustment of the body is needed. [See Photo Series 13-2(C).]

Hands

The palms are facing out from the body in the ready position or where the ball is. The hands cushion the ball into the stomach and chest. The coach should listen for two rapid sounds as the ball makes contact with the hands first and the stomach and chest second. For balls that are taken in the chest there is a wedging action as the ball is held firm between the chest and hands. If the ball is driven hard into the chest the hands will make immediate contact as soon as the ball connects with the chest.

Feet

The feet are positioned in a balanced stance, shoulder width apart. Raising the body on the toes allows quick movements across the goal.

Stopping Shots—Above the Body

A ball that is played above the goalkeeper's head requires that both hands be positioned quickly, as now the body cannot be used to protect the goal. [See Photo Series 13-2(D) and (E).]

Hands

The hands are relaxed with the fingers spread. A "W" shape is formed as both thumbs are placed close together. This allows a wide surface area of the hands to be placed on a large surface area of the ball. Young players find it difficult to form this "W" due to the small size of their hands, so it is best to place emphasis on the goalkeeper's positioning both hands behind the ball to hold on to it. After the ball is caught, it is brought down and hugged into the chest area for protection.

Feet

The feet are spread shoulder width apart. If the goalkeeper has to leave the ground to catch the ball, a driving action is performed by putting one knee up into the chest. This allows for more height than a two-footed takeoff and also offers protection against challenging players.

Stopping Shots—Away From the Body: Diving

A goalkeeper who positions himself correctly will deny the opposing player the opportunity to place the ball past him. Situations do occur in which a goalkeeper must leave his basic stance and use his body to obstruct a shot by diving.

For shots that are played low around his body, the goalkeeper must move the upper part of his body down quickly to the ball. A goalkeeper can use his feet whenever possible. The low hand position of the basic stance assists in this task.

For shots that are placed wide of the body an effort must be made to move the body across to the ball immediately. The goalkeeper must then decide whether to hold on to the ball or whether to deflect it away.

Ground Shots

The body weight is placed on the leg closest to the ball. A pushing-off on this leg then follows toward the ball. [See Photo Series 13-2(F) through (H).]

Hands

The hands each have a different function for the ground shot. One hand is placed directly behind the ball to take the pace off it, while the other hand secures the ball by being placed on top of it. The arms then bring the ball back into the chest area for added protection.

Feet

The feet must move quickly for the body to thrust itself across the intended direction of the shot. A sideways skipping action occurs when a goalkeeper moves laterally across the goal. This permits the shifting of weight from one leg to the other to be carried out more smoothly as the dive begins from the leg closest to the ball.

High Shots

The spectacular goalkeeper thrives on the opportunity to throw himself through the air. This skill is often required during a game and therefore should be taught with the basics. [See Photo Series 13-2(I) and (J).]

**PHOTO SERIES 13-2
GOALKEEPING TECHNIQUE: STOPPING SHOTS
(Cont'd)**

**DIVING ACROSS THE GOAL TO SAVE A
GROUND SHOT AWAY FROM THE BODY**

(F)

(G)

(H)

Hands

The hands are held in the same position as for the ground shot. Once the ball is caught, it is brought into the body for protection or wedged between the hands and the ground. A goalkeeper's vision should be unobstructed throughout his dive, and he should attempt to view the ball through both arms. If the ball is to be deflected over the crossbar one hand is used to turn it over. If the ball has not been hit hard, the fingertips can be used to scoop the ball up and over. For more powerful shots the fingers and palms are used together. All shots that are to be deflected must be placed wide of the goal and out of play.

PHOTO SERIES 13-2
GOALKEEPING TECHNIQUE: STOPPING SHOTS
(Cont'd)

HIGH SHOTS

(I)
Saving a High Shot
Away From the Body

(J)
Deflecting the
Ball Over the
Crossbar

Feet

The feet move sideways from a balanced position and thrust the body across to the ball. The leg closest to the shot generates the initial thrust, as this leg bends before extending into the ball.

Dealing With Crosses

If a goalkeeper is going to catch a ball that is played in from the wing, he has to possess confidence not only in his own ability but also in the defenders around him. When a goalkeeper has made up his mind to take the ball there is no turning back. Indecision at this moment can lead to drastic results. A goalkeeper's dominance of the goal area is easily seen in the manner with which he deals with crosses.

Defenders have to allow the goalkeeper the time and space to react to the ball unhindered. Once he has called for the ball he should be given every opportunity to carry out his intentions. If there is no call from the goalkeeper, then the play has to be destroyed by these defenders.

In stopping a ball played down the wing and across the goal area, a goalkeeper must be correctly positioned, able to judge when to move, and then quick and sure in committing himself. Only in this way can he function effectively in dealing with crosses.

The following three areas, then, will be covered in this discussion:

- Positioning for the cross
- Judging
- Committing

Positioning for the Cross

A ball can be played from any area on the wing and from any distance, therefore a goalkeeper must position himself at different points within the goal area. No matter where this ball is played from, the goalkeeper must be aware of where he is positioned in relation to:

- The ball
- The near post—the post closest to the ball

The ball that is played from a long distance allows the goalkeeper more time to position himself correctly. If the ball is played from the area around the corner flag, the position of the goalkeeper will be different from the one he would take for a ball played from the midfield area. The near post is used as a guide for positioning against a cross. A goalkeeper should never be beaten at the near post.

Visual knowledge of where this near post is located can be as effective as physically touching it. The area inside this near post has to be protected at all times because, since it is the closest distance between the ball and the goal, it is the most accessible area for the attacking player to use. A ball that is played across the goal allows the goalkeeper more time than can be found in the near-post cross. (See Diagrams 13-1 and 13-2.) The basic stance that was discussed earlier is also used when preparing to deal with crosses, the major difference being that the body is now turned toward the intended cross. A clear view of the immediate surroundings is especially important as now attacking players are looking to move across the goalkeeper to obstruct his view.

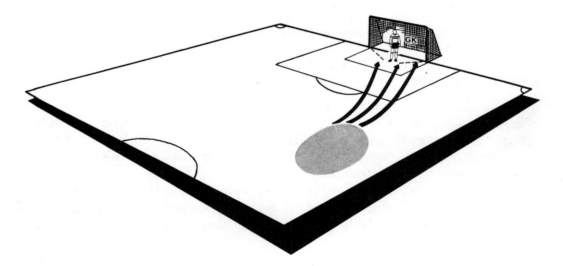

DIAGRAM 13-1
For a ball that is played from the shaded area the goalkeeper positions himself a few yards away from the goal line and close to the middle of the goal.

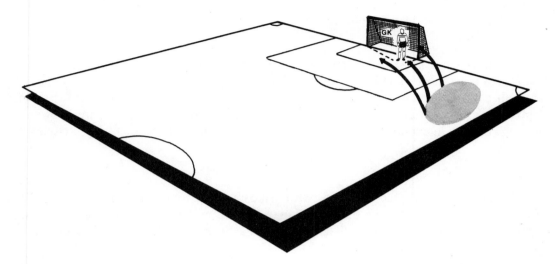

DIAGRAM 13-2

For a ball played from the shaded area the goalkeeper positions himself one yard away from the goal line and four yards from the near post. As the ball comes closer to the goal line, the cross to the near-post area is more of a threat, and therefore it must be covered by the goalkeeper.

Judging

When a goalkeeper is correctly positioned he must wait until the ball is kicked before making his move. The chances of error are increased when a goalkeeper tries prematurely to anticipate where a cross is intended to go. He must judge:

- The direction of the ball
- The speed of the ball

Once the goalkeeper has judged the ball he must then act quickly upon his judgment. There are then two decisions to be made. The goalkeeper can either:

- Stay on his goal line, or
- Move out to take the cross

Any ball that is played into the six-yard area or up to the penalty spot is the goalkeeper's personal responsibility. The decision has already been made. He must take charge of the situation by calling loud and clear: "Keepers." Communicating with teammates in the goal area can aid immensely in preventing the mass confusion that usually accompanies balls played in this area. Goalkeepers should not assist the attacking team in their task of causing confusion for the defense. If there is doubt in the goalkeeper's mind as to whether he should move out to take the ball, the decision would be to remain on the goal line and leave the responsibility of clearing the ball with the defenders.

Committing

If the goalkeeper elects to take the cross himself he must:

- Inform the defenders of his intentions
- Move to the ball

• Catch the ball at the highest point

• Punch the ball

Some coaches insist that a goalkeeper make his move early. This is not the case. A goalkeeper must move quickly only after he has assessed the direction and speed of the ball. The ball cannot be brought down any faster than gravity will allow, therefore time is on a goalkeeper's side especially when it is a high cross. After the defenders are made aware of the goalkeeper's intentions through his verbal information, then the goalkeeper begins his function.

Moving to the Ball

By moving quickly, the goalkeeper will make up for the time he used to assess the flight of the ball. If he can move into the ball's line of flight it will help in the timing of his jump. However, this is difficult to do. The goalkeeper's timing can be thrown off due to the inability to track the ball.

Catching the Ball at the Highest Point

The fact that the goalkeeper can use his hands is never more obvious than in the confrontation with attacking players who challenge in the air. A one-footed takeoff is used to gain maximum height. [See Photo Series 13-2(K).] This type of takeoff is productive because:

• It can be performed in stride.

• It allows a smooth transfer of body weight from a forward run into an upward thrust.

• It can be used to provide protection for the body as the driving leg moves up toward the chest.

**PHOTO SERIES 13-2
GOALKEEPING TECHNIQUE: STOPPING SHOTS
(Cont'd)**

**(K)
Moving to Catch the
Ball at the Highest
Point**

The arms are outstretched above and slightly in front of the head. Once the ball has been caught, it should be brought down and tucked into the chest as soon as possible.

Punching the Ball

When the goalkeeper is surrounded by players he can elect to punch the ball away. This occurs when he is unsure of handling the ball soundly. There are two methods of punching the ball:

- One-fisted
- Two-fisted

Both are effective when used in the correct situation. [See Photo Series 13-2(L) and (M).]

One-Fisted

This is performed by the arm closest to the goal as the goalkeeper strikes the ball across the line of flight. The fist should connect through the lower half of the ball.

Two-Fisted

This is performed with two fists striking the ball through the lower half. It is productive when the goalkeeper is in the direct path of the ball.

PHOTO SERIES 13-2
GOALKEEPING TECHNIQUE: STOPPING SHOTS
(Cont'd)

PUNCHING SHOTS

(L)
One-Fisted Punch

(M)
Two-Fisted Punch

Both punching techniques must be performed with the intention of clearing the ball through:

- Height–allowing the defenders to reorganize
- Distance–away from the immediate area around the goal
- Width–away from the congested area in the middle of the field

Positioning

Goalkeepers are constantly adjusting their position. It is therefore important that they have an understanding of why one position is more appropriate for a situation than another. The goalkeeper must assess:

- The position of the ball, both in terms of the distance and the angle
- The movements of the player with the ball—whether he will shoot or hold on to the ball

After these have been assessed, the goalkeeper can begin his response to the oncoming threat. He reacts by:

- Positioning his body in a direct line between the ball and the middle of the goal. This may vary slightly in some situations.
- Holding his basic stance if the attacker is prepared to shoot. The problem that most goalkeepers encounter is in their movement forward while diving. His position must be set and balanced.
- Moving out toward the ball if the attacker pushes the ball too far ahead. This should be done quickly and with control.
- Moving out to challenge the attacker. If the goalkeeper moves out too fast and too quickly, the ball can be chipped over him. If he does not move out at all, a shot can be taken with most of the goal exposed.

When the goalkeeper moves away from the goal in order to challenge for the ball he must:

- Present an obstacle to the attacker by making his body as large as possible.
- Not anticipate where the player will move or if he will take the shot. A goalkeeper must react to the ball.
- Spread his body across the intended path of the ball if he has decided to go for the ball. Young players familiar with sliding into base in baseball will attempt the same skill toward an attacker. It then becomes easy for the attacker to place the ball past the advancing goalkeeper. Timing again becomes important in this skill.

Correct positioning techniques for the goalkeeper are described and illustrated in Diagrams 13-3 through 13-9 and in Photo Series 13-3(A) through (E).

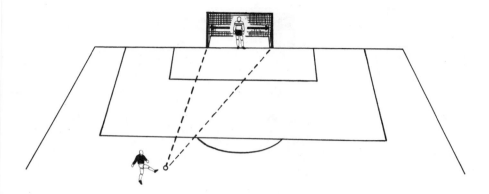

DIAGRAM 13-3

By staying on the goal line, the goalkeeper allows the attacker a wider area of goal to shoot at.

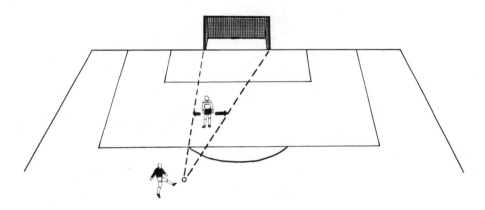

DIAGRAM 13-4

Goalkeeper's controlled advance narrows down the shooting angle of the attacker.

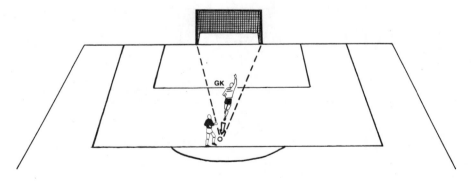

DIAGRAM 13-5

By sliding out, feet first, goalkeeper gives an attacker the opportunity to place the ball alongside the advancing goalkeeper's body with relative ease.

DIAGRAM 13-6

Goalkeeper's advance, with his body placed across the path of the ball, allows little opportunity for the attacker to move the ball beyond the goalkeeper.

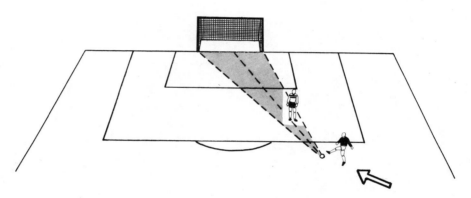

DIAGRAM 13-7

Illustration shows correct positioning for the goalkeeper after he has moved out at different angles to the left of goal.

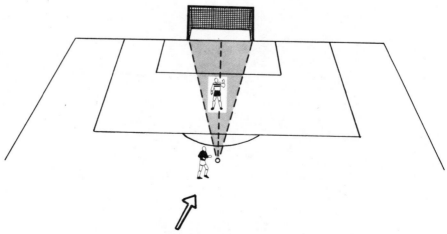

DIAGRAM 13-8

Illustration shows correct positioning for the goalkeeper after he has moved out from the goal at different angles.

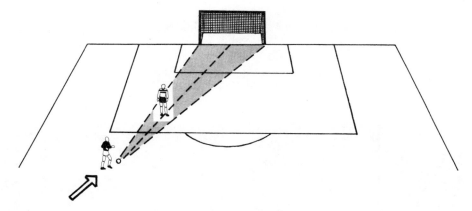

DIAGRAM 13-9
Illustration shows correct positioning for the goalkeeper after he has moved out at different angles to the right of goal.

PHOTO SERIES 13-3
GOALKEEPING TECHNIQUE: POSITIONING

MOVING OUT TO NARROW THE ANGLE

(A)

(B)

PHOTO SERIES 13-3
GOALKEEPING TECHNIQUE: POSITIONING
(Cont'd)

SPREADING THE BODY ACROSS
THE PATH OF THE ATTACKER

(C)

(D)

(E)

Distribution

Possession is either maintained or regained once the goalkeeper has the ball. It is counterproductive to immediately give up this possession through careless distribution of the ball. It can also be very damaging to give up the ball in the defending third of the field especially in and around the penalty area.

Constructive distribution by the goalkeeper is as important on offense as saving a shot is on defense. This transitional phase of the game from defense to offense must be made with relative ease as the goalkeeper initiates an attack instead of merely clearing the ball.

Once the goalkeeper has the ball in his possession his first priority is to look down the middle of the field for an open player. This is the most direct route to goal but it is also the most dangerous as players normally congest this area. Nevertheless, this route must still be given top priority even though the goalkeeper may not pursue it.

The second choice is to look down the wings for an open player. This is the safest form of distribution if players are available for the pass. Space can be utilized on the wings when players begin to make runs from the middle out wide. Whichever choice is made, the primary concern is for the pass to arrive at its destination with little or no threat of interception. If there is any doubt, the surest pass is the short one to a teammate who is close by.

There are three forms of distribution:

- Throwing
- Volley kick
- Goal kick

Throwing

Accuracy is more attainable when a goalkeeper uses his hands rather than his feet. The further the throw the more difficult it is to reach the target player; therefore a goalkeeper must be aware of his physical limitations.

Overarm Throw

The body is positioned sideways toward the intended receiver, with the ball held in the palm of the hand. One arm begins to move forward in an arc shape while the opposite arm is held out in front of the body and then brought down to balance the throwing arm.

The legs are spread wide for a balanced position throughout the movement. The goalkeeper can release the ball at different stages through the arc. If the ball is intended to be played directly into the feet of a teammate who is positioned relatively close, the release will be late. This allows the ball to be played close to the ground in an effort to make control easier for the player receiving the ball. If the ball is to be played over a longer distance, the release will be made earlier to provide height for the pass.

Underarm Throw

The ball is played from the hand closest to the ground. This bowling action presents few control problems for the player receiving it. It is used over short distances where the path from the goalkeeper to his teammate is clear.

Continually stress the value of throwing the ball. If used correctly, it is the surest means of retaining possession. Kicking the ball presents a 50-50 situation for all players involved in receiving this kick. Why decrease the odds of maintaining possession through using a skill that is very often inappropriate for the majority of situations?

Volley Kick

This is often referred to as punting the ball. It is used over long distances as a means of clearing the ball instead of building possession soccer with it. If used correctly it is productive from a tactical standpoint. When a 1 vs. 1 situation has developed down the field, a volley kick over the congested area can be productive. It is also effective on a windy day when the wind is working in favor of the goalkeeper.

The ball is dropped from hands held out in front of the body at waist height. The instep makes contact through the lower part of the ball. After contact has been made, the kicking leg continues through the ball. Lifting the whole body up into the air assists with achieving more distance on the kick.

Some goalkeepers prefer to make contact with the ball as it touches the ground—called a half-volley. If the result is favorable and the goalkeeper feels comfortable doing this, it should be encouraged. The biggest problem associated with the half-volley concerns the increased chance of error that accompanies reliance on ground conditions. Uneven fields present many difficulties for players, especially in and around the goal area.

Goal Kick

The main advantage of distributing a stationary ball is in the time that is available to perform the technique correctly. This however, can also be a disadvantage as the amount of time available also allows the opposition to catch up on their marking responsibilities. If a goalkeeper has poor form in striking the ball, another outfield player can be used until you have worked with the goalkeeper on this weakness. This should be employed only occasionally as the opposition immediately begins with a numerical advantage.

The technique for striking the ball is the same as that used for the drive pass. The major difference is to be found in the contact area on the ball. Emphasis is now placed on striking through the lower half of the ball rather than through the middle. The body should lift off the ground during the follow-through stage of the kick.

The goalkeeper possesses unique abilities. These should be harnessed to the fullest through understanding and accepting the fact that the goalkeeper is different and should be treated as such.

DRILLS

DRILL #1

| PLAYING POSITION: 1ST MAN OFFENSE/GOALKEEPING |

| COACHING LEVEL: WITHOUT OPPOSITION |

| KEY COACHING POINTS: CORRECT TECHNIQUE FOR STOPPING SHOTS, POSITIONING, & DISTRIBUTION |

All shooting drills can be applied toward the coaching of the goalkeeper. Portable goals should be used at every opportunity.

Balls Played Into the Body

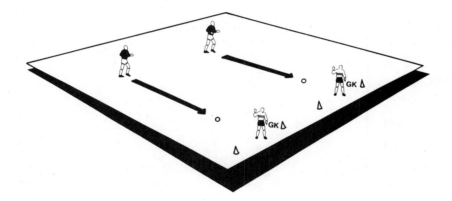

DIAGRAM 13-10

Goalkeepers can work in pairs, or outfield players can assist in the drill. (See Diagram 13-10.) The ball is rolled to the goalkeeper along the ground. The emphasis is placed on:

- The Ready Position
- The Long Barrier Technique
- The Scoop Technique

Balls can be varied into the stomach, chest, and above the head. At this point you should stress the correct use of the hands and feet.

Balls Played Away From the Body—Diving

The ball is now played to the side of the goalkeeper along the ground, as shown in Diagram 13-11. The goalkeeper can adopt a kneeling position to begin with before assuming a crouching position and finally the ready position. The emphasis is placed on:

DIAGRAM 13-11

- The hands
- The feet

Once the goalkeeper is proficient in dealing with ground shots, the serve can be directed through the air. This diving action can also begin from the kneeling position. The emphasis is now placed on:

- The hands
- The feet
- The takeoff
- The landing

You must be aware of the goalkeeper's landing procedure. If the goalkeeper is continually landing incorrectly, not only does he fail to improve but a serious injury could develop.

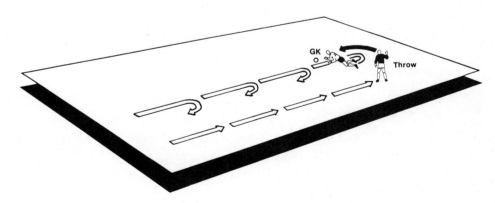

DIAGRAM 13-12

An excellent reaction drill for a ball that is brought back across the goalkeeper's body can be found in the reverse side-step. (See Diagram 13-12.) Move sideways with the goalkeeper, while facing him. The ball is then served behind and to the side of the goalkeeper. He must quickly change direction in an attempt to stop the ball. Situations similar to this occur in a game when a shot is placed into the goal area and at the last moment is deflected back across the goalkeeper's body as he is following the initial shot.

Vary the serve both low and high and also play some balls in the same direction that the goalkeeper is moving. This forces the goalkeeper to be alert at all times. The emphasis is placed on:

- Quick side-stepping movements
- Quick turns
- Sound handling

Crosses and Punching

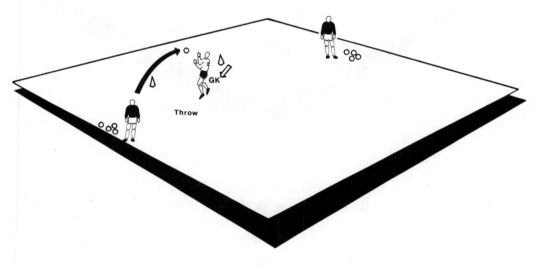

DIAGRAM 13-13

The ball is served from the hands through the air for the goalkeeper to react to, as shown in Diagram 13-13. At this early stage the emphasis is placed on:

- Positioning for the cross
- Judging
- Handling

If the goalkeeper has problems with his takeoff he can be taught to practice skipping. Here you should stress the one-footed takeoff and the driving up of the other leg to the chest. Then check to see whether the goalkeeper is selecting the wrong leg for taking off. It is usually the nonkicking leg that is used to initiate this upward movement.

Balls can be played from different angles. Once the goalkeeper becomes proficient in the basics of handling a cross the emphasis can be placed on catching the ball at the highest point, an area that many youngsters find difficulty with. Their tendency all too often is to bend their arms and catch the ball close to the head. When opponents are introduced, however, they will quickly realize the importance of stretching above the heads of threatening attackers.

A variation of this drill is to allow the goalkeeper the opportunity to punch the ball with one fist and then with two fists. Balls can again be served from different angles.

Positioning

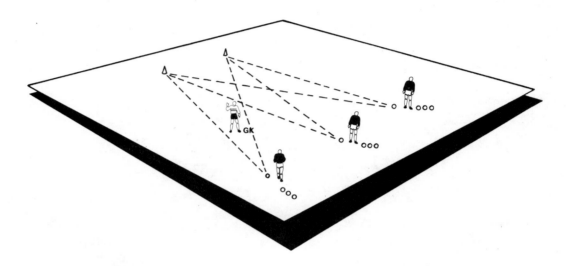

DIAGRAM 13-14

Three players are positioned at different angles with a supply of balls. (See Diagram 13-14.) The goalkeeper rotates around to work with each player. The player with the ball makes a run toward the goal at half-speed. The goalkeeper then leaves his goal and approaches the attacker before positioning himself correctly for the shot. When the goalkeeper becomes proficient in his task, the speed of the player's run can be increased.

Emphasis is placed on:

- The position of the goalkeeper in relation to the ball and the goal
- The ready position
- The timing of his run from goal

You can develop this drill so the goalkeeper practices coming out of the goal to challenge the attacker by spreading his body across the path of the ball. The attacking player must allow the goalkeeper to win every ball until there is sufficient improvement in the fundamentals of the technique.

Distribution

The goalkeeper can work on throwing or kicking to different areas of the field, as shown in Diagram 13-15. Target areas in front of or behind players can be marked off. The emphasis is placed on:

- Accuracy

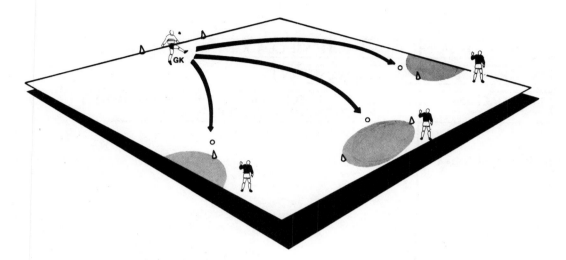

DIAGRAM 13-15

DRILL #2

PLAYING POSITION: 1ST MAN OFFENSE/GOALKEEPING

COACHING LEVEL: PASSIVE OPPOSITION

KEY COACHING POINTS: CORRECT TECHNIQUE FOR STOPPING SHOTS, POSITIONING, & DISTRIBUTION

Balls Played Into the Body

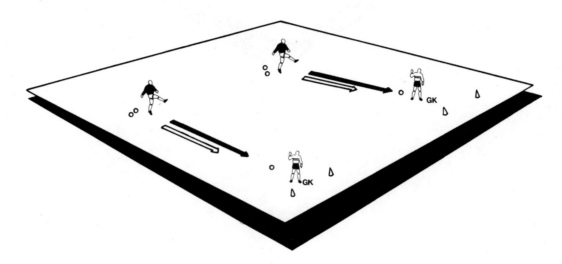

DIAGRAM 13-16

As illustrated in Diagram 13-16, an outfield player takes a shot directly at the goalkeeper. As soon as the ball has been released the attacker follows up on his shot to distract the goalkeeper. Any ball that rebounds off the goalkeeper's body is still live and can be treated as such by both players. The shots can be varied to include high, low, and bouncing balls. The emphasis is placed on:

• Holding on to the ball.

Balls Played Away From the Body—Diving

A distracting player runs across the face of the goal as a shot is being taken by another player. (See Diagram 13-17.) The player taking the shot again follows up to recover any loose balls. The position of the distracting player in relation to the goalkeeper varies according to the proficiency of the goalkeeper. The more capable he is in holding on to the ball, the closer this player can be placed.

The goalkeeper can practice reacting to a ball that changes direction at the last moment by placing large sturdy cones in front of the goal, as in Diagram 13-18. The goalkeeper is positioned behind these and must react quickly to the deflected shot which was aimed into the cone area. If cones are unavailable, players can be used to deflect the ball.

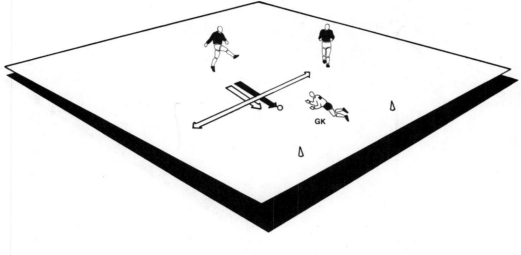

DIAGRAM 13-17

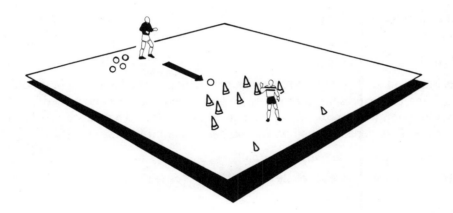

DIAGRAM 13-18

The emphasis is placed on:

- A quick change of direction
- Sound handling

Crosses and Punching

A ball is played high into the goal area from the wing. (See Diagram 13-19.) The goalkeeper must challenge a passive player who jumps up with him. Only slight physical contact can be made. If the ball is mishandled the passive player can react by taking a shot. The emphasis is placed on:

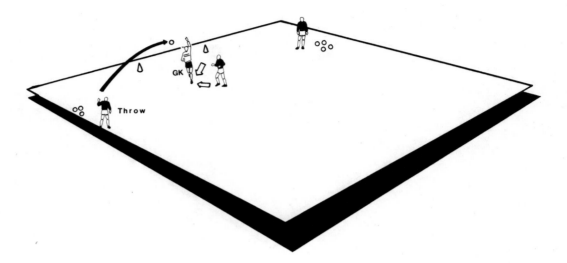

DIAGRAM 13-19

- Positioning for the cross
- Judging
- Handling

It is important at this stage to reemphasize catching the ball at the highest point, as now the challenging player presents a problem. A one-footed takeoff is now used.

A progression to punching can be included in the drill. The choice of whether to use one fist or two fists depends upon where the ball is played from.

- One fist—across the path of the ball
- Two fists—into the path of the ball

Positioning

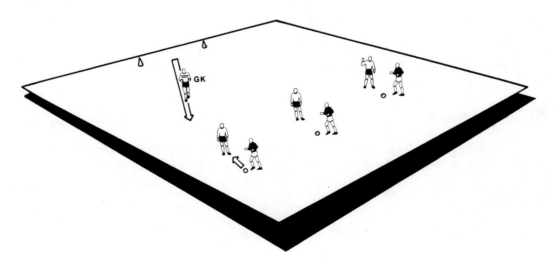

DIAGRAM 13-20

Three attacking players are positioned against three passive defenders. (See Diagram 13-20.) One attacker challenges a defender and beats him. As soon as the defender is beaten, the goalkeeper must react to the situation. The goalkeeper should decide whether to:

- Stay on his line
- Advance out and position himself
- Advance out and challenge for the ball

The emphasis is placed on:

- Dealing with the situation in the correct way

Distribution

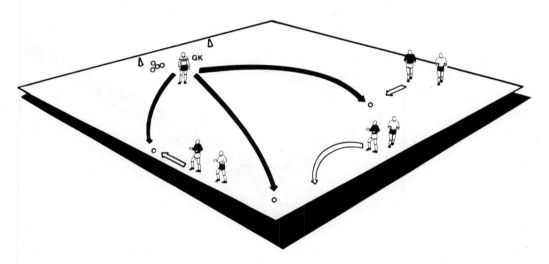

DIAGRAM 13-21

The goalkeeper must pass the ball out to one of three teammates who are marked by defenders, as illustrated in Diagram 13-21. These defenders should be close enough to offer a distraction without presenting any physical challenge. This "shadowing" effect will force the goalkeeper to find the attacking player who has created more space within which to work. The attacking players must work to get open.

DRILL #3

PLAYING POSITION: 1ST MAN OFFENSE/GOALKEEPING

COACHING LEVEL: POSITIVE OPPOSITION

KEY COACHING POINTS: WHEN & WHERE TO REACT

Balls Played Into and Away From the Body—Diving

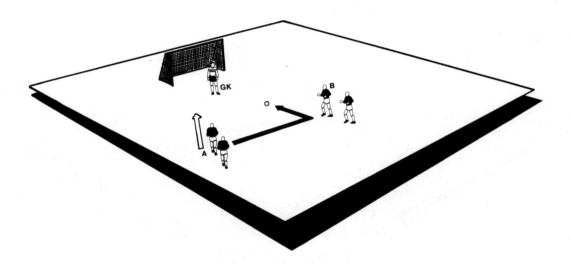

DIAGRAM 13-22

A goalkeeper is placed in a portable goal. Two lines of attacking players are positioned in front and to the side of the goal, as shown in Diagram 13-22. Player A passes the ball to player B who takes a shot. Player A moves in toward the goalkeeper to take advantage of any mistake he may make. The goalkeeper must position himself first against player A and then move across to react to player B's shot. The shots will vary both in speed, direction, and height.

The emphasis is placed on:

- Correct form
- Sure handling
- Correct decision making

This drill progresses to either player's taking the shot under different circumstances. The goalkeeper must prepare for a shot to be taken at any time and from any area.

Crosses and Punching

A goalkeeper is placed in goal with a defender and an attacker close by. (See Diagram 13-23.) Four servers are positioned at different angles and varying distances from the goal. One ball is played into the goal area where the goalkeeper challenges the attacking player while communicating with the defending player.

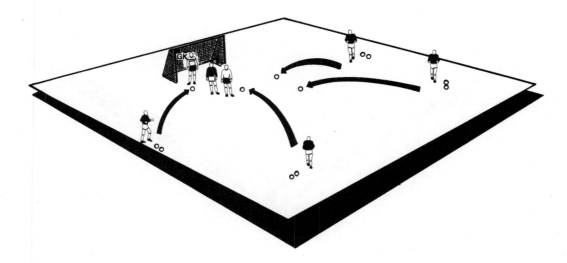

DIAGRAM 13-23

Decision making begins to play a major role at this point as the goalkeeper determines whether to:

- Stay on the goal line
- Advance out to catch the ball
- Advance out to punch the ball

These decisions are based on:

- Where the ball arrives
- When the ball arrives
- Where other players are positioned

More players can be added to the drill at the appropriate stage in the goalkeeper's development.

Positioning

A triangle is arranged, with three cones placed 10 yards from each other. A group of players forms a large circle around the cones, as in Diagram 13-24, and passes the ball among themselves. The goalkeeper moves within the triangle to cover the three goals. Every opportunity should be taken to place the ball into the corner of the goal. A supply of balls is made available to the attackers.

Three goals are arranged in a triangle with a goalkeeper in each. (See Diagram 13-25.) The distance will vary with the skill level of the goalkeepers. Each goalkeeper has a supply of balls next to the goal. The drill begins with one goalkeeper throwing or volleying a ball from his goal to one of the other two. If the goalkeeper saves the ball he can continue with the drill in the same way choosing one of the other goals as his target. A point is awarded for every goal scored. If the shot is wide on one goal, the goalkeeper from that goal will use another ball to continue the drill.

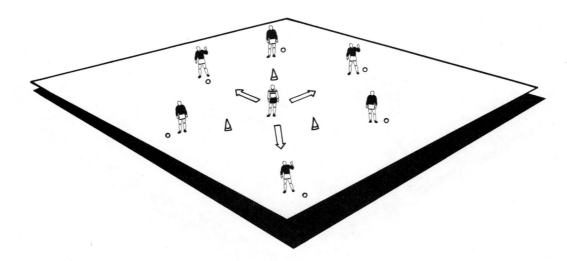

DIAGRAM 13-24

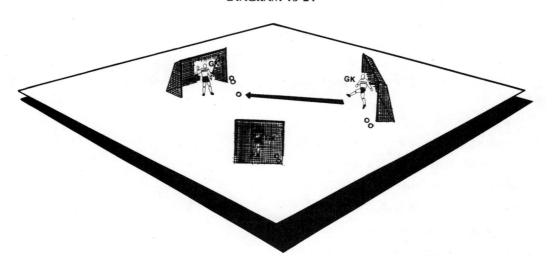

DIAGRAM 13-25

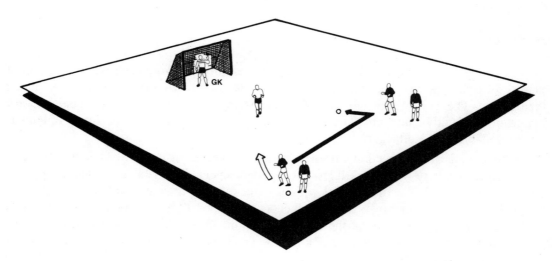

DIAGRAM 13-26

A 2 vs. 1 situation develops when two attackers move the ball down the field toward a defender. (See Diagram 13-26.) The goalkeeper must react according to the outcome of the challenge by the defender. Verbal information is given by the goalkeeper to assist the defender.

Distribution

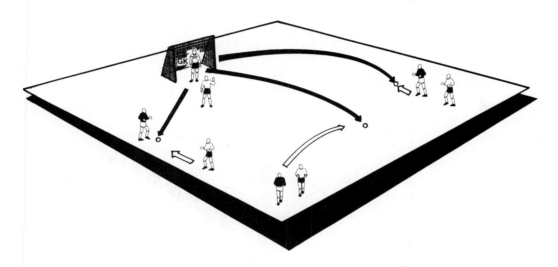

DIAGRAM 13-27

Defenders now have to mark the attackers tightly all over the field. An additional defender is placed in front of the goalkeeper to provide immediate distraction. (See Diagram 13-27.) The attacking players should attempt to lose their respective defenders and open up certain areas of the field. The goalkeeper must be alert and ready to play the ball quickly once such an opening has been created. It is unproductive for a goalkeeper to merely clear the ball without any prior thought.

DRILL #4

PLAYING POSITION: 1ST MAN OFFENSE/GOALKEEPING

COACHING LEVEL: SMALL-SIDED GAME

KEY COACHING POINTS: WHEN & WHERE TO REACT

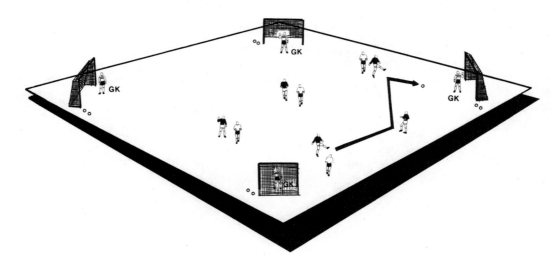

DIAGRAM 13-28

A small-sided game of 5 vs. 5 with four goals and four goalkeepers provides many of the situations which a goalkeeper has to contend with in a game. (See Diagram 13-28.) The advantage of using four goals is that many shots can be taken and many saves attempted. Once the goalkeeper has the ball in his possession he passes it to the team that failed to take the shot. A shot cannot be taken by the receiving team directly back at the goalkeeper who just gave them the ball. All aspects of goalkeeping can be covered.

DIAGRAM 13-29

Two portable goals are used with two goalkeepers, as shown in Diagram 13-29. A 3 vs. 3 takes place in a defined area by one line. Players can pass the ball between themselves only in their defending half. Once they play the ball forward across this line a shot must be taken by the player receiving the pass. All aspects of goalkeeping can be covered.

DRILL #5

| PLAYING POSITION: 1ST MAN OFFENSE |

| COACHING LEVEL: TEAM TACTICS |

| KEY COACHING POINTS: ASPECTS OF GOALKEEPING THAT NEED TO BE STRESSED |

Very few tactical plays include the goalkeeper. He can be used to begin a tactical ploy or he can be used to deny one. He is a casual observer of his own team's buildup and an instrumental object in disrupting the opposition. If he fails in either, the consequences can be damaging.

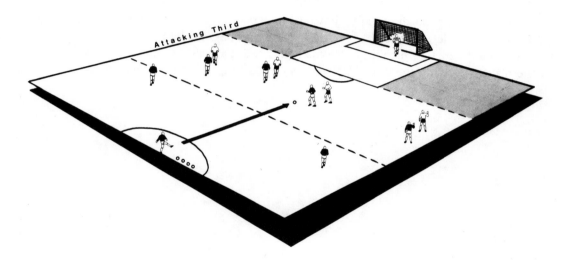

DIAGRAM 13-30

In one-half of the field seven offensive players compete against four defenders, as shown in Diagram 13-30. The teams are evenly matched in the attacking third with a 4 vs. 4. The three remaining attackers are positioned in the middle of the field and used as support players. The offensive team must work the ball up into the corners of the field which are marked off. When the ball enters one of these areas only one offensive player is permitted to follow. The ball can then be crossed into the goal area for the goalkeeper to practice taking crosses and distributing the ball back out to the midfield area.

CHAPTER 14

SET PLAYS

COACHING POINTS

Defending at Set Plays

With so many goals being scored from set plays (throw-ins, corner kicks, and free kicks), there is a serious need to look at the defensive principles involved with this aspect of the game. The attacking team has two distinct advantages at any set play:

- They have possession.
- They have a plan.

There is little that a defense can do to totally overcome these two factors. What a defense can do is to have a sense of organization and concentration as soon as the set play has been acknowledged. If a defense can be taught that both organization and concentration are paramount to their success in a set play situation, then the scales become more evenly balanced.

Individual players must be aware of their own roles and the roles of their teammates. Discipline is important, as the outcome of a set play depends directly on the necessary procedures being carried out thoroughly. If a team is organized soundly on defense then the task of the offense becomes more difficult to accomplish. On defense it is important that coach and team understand the relationship of the following elements:

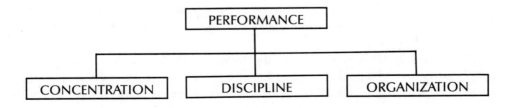

All set plays require a team to:

- Prevent the direct shot
- Cover space
- Mark players

The determining factors in making a choice of whether to cover space or mark players are the location on the field where the set play occurs and the position of the opposing team.

Free Kicks

A team that is awarded a free kick usually knows what they want to accomplish. It may be a direct shot on goal, a short pass to a teammate, or a long pass down the field. Whatever their intention, the free kick is usually taken quickly to disrupt a defense's concentration.

A disciplined defense should likewise act quickly by not allowing the ball to move on a direct path to goal. The kick has to be challenged immediately by a defensive player who blocks the shot. A defensive wall can then be formed to prevent any further threat on goal. The number of players who take up position in the wall is again determined by where on the field the ball is placed.

Delaying the attack allows time for the defense to get organized to cover the space alongside and behind the defense as well as to mark threatening players.

Setting Up the Wall

The reason a wall is set up is primarily to defend one area of the goal while the goalkeeper defends the other area. A wall is vitally important for defense against a free kick near the penalty area. Its purpose is to defend the area closest to the near post by reducing the threat of a direct shot on goal.

The speed at which a wall is set up is determined by how well the defense is organized to combat the major problem that normally occurs—confusion.

Where to Set Up the Wall

Positioning a wall should not be the responsibility of the goalkeeper, even though the blame is often shouldered by the goalkeeper if there is a breakdown in the organization of the wall. A goalkeeper who attempts to set up a wall can be distracted from his main responsibility, which is to position quickly to respond to a quick shot. A goalkeeper who rushes from one post to the other in a panic move, to ensure that his wall is correctly positioned, exposes the entire goal to the offense. He should be in a central position to see the ball, but not where he is behind the wall. This central position will obviously depend on how many players are in the wall and where they are positioned. In Diagrams 14-1 and 14-2 the wall is positioned at the near post with the goalkeeper covering the far side of the goal in a central position. The four-man defensive wall is set up to protect the right half of the goal. This is to prevent the right-footed player from striking a ball that normally curves inward. (See Diagram 14-3.) If it is known that the player taking the free kick is left-footed, the wall should protect the left half of the goal.

Some degree of order is required for a defensive set play. It begins with the goalkeeper. Immediately after the referee has awarded a free kick, the goalkeeper must determine exactly where the kick will be taken from. After he has determined this, the goalkeeper calls

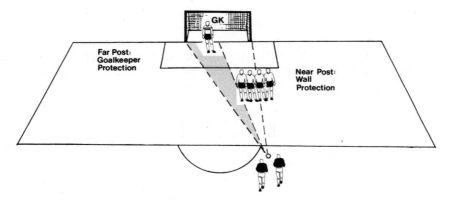

DIAGRAM 14-1

This four-man defensive wall is set up to protect the near post from a free kick on the right side.

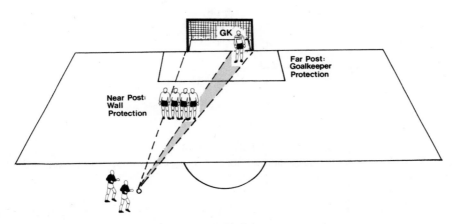

DIAGRAM 14-2

This four-man defensive wall is set up to protect the near post from a free kick on the left side.

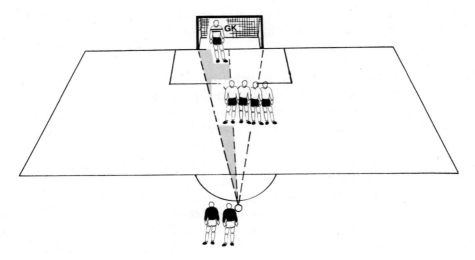

DIAGRAM 14-3

This four-man defensive wall is set up to protect the right side of the goal when the ball is directly in the middle of the goal.

out a number, loud and clear. This tells the defense the number of players that should be in the wall and is needed quickly so the correct number of players can move into position.

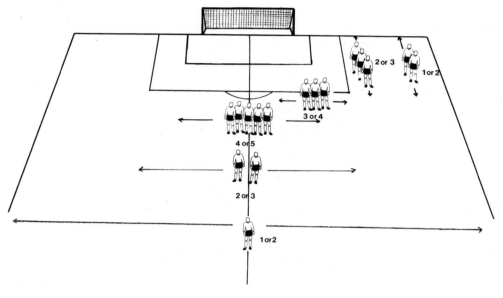

DIAGRAM 14-4

Illustration shows the suggested number of players to position in the wall from different angles.

Diagram 14-4 shows the number of players to be placed in the wall from different angles. The team as a whole has to be aware that the goalkeeper is given the responsibility of calling out a number and that they must respond to it. Obviously, the goalkeeper must understand this responsibility. Stress the urgency with which a defensive team must organize. It is a mistake to place too many players in a wall due to the one-sided numerical advantage of the offensive team. Once a wall is set up with the minimum number of players— one—then the offensive team begins with an advantage.

Players in the Wall

Once a number has been called, the defense immediately follows this command. An outfield player positions himself behind the ball and then directs only one player in the wall. This player is the near-post player. Selecting the players to be in the wall ahead of time can help eliminate the areas of confusion as players have specific roles to perform. The designated near-post player will position himself slightly over the line drawn from the ball to the near post. This will help prevent a ball from being bent around the wall. Once the near-post player is set he should not move. The remaining players in the wall then position themselves on the inside of him. (See Diagram 14-5.)

An alternative to this prior selection setup can be that the first player in the wall becomes the player who takes up the near-post position. The players who arrive immediately after him take up the remaining positions which have not been predetermined. The

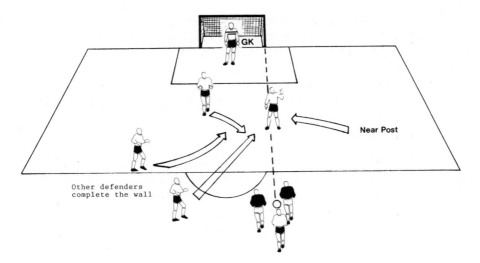

DIAGRAM 14-5
Defender directs the near-post player in the wall; other defenders complete the
wall.

advantages to this latter approach concern the need to have players in the wall quickly, without
having to check if any of the wall players are off the field at the time the free kick is awarded.
The disadvantage to not having predetermined assignments can be found when the wall
contains players who are more suited for other defensive positions.

Tall players are more suited to positions where they can play to their strength of clearing
the ball with their heads. Wing fullbacks are also more suited to defending against the threat
of an attack from down the wings, especially if the free kick is taken in the middle.

It should be noted that:

- Tall players, if in the wall, should cover the near post.
- Players should raise their bodies slightly by standing on their toes. This will add a few
  extra inches to the wall and also allow players to move away quickly should the wall
  have to break. The legs should be spread sufficiently to provide a stable base with no
  sizable gaps visible.
- Players should protect themselves below the stomach area by crossing the hands.
- Players should lower their heads to allow vision of the ball while still protecting the
  face.
- Players should not link in a wall. A breaking player may not be able to perform his job
  if he is held back. This also limits protection.
- Players should not stand with their backs to the ball. This provides better protection,
  but it is at the expense of the players' ability to watch and react to developing play.

On free kicks around the penalty area when there are four players in the wall, an
additional "speedster" can be placed directly in front of the wall. His function is to attack the
ball as soon as it is touched by the offense. This is more effective when it is an indirect free

kick and additional time is available to close down the shot. The fastest player in the team will be the most successful here. The number of players called for by the goalkeeper is only for the wall itself. This extra defender is not included in the call.

On an indirect free kick a ball that is played wide provides the wall with the necessary information on which to base its next move. A wall must break from its original position in one direction—toward the ball. Narrowing the shooting angle prevents an easy shot on goal.

Players Not in the Wall

If too many players are placed in the wall the numerical advantage is presented to the opposition. When a free kick is awarded around the penalty area all ten players must recover into the area between the ball and the goal to seal off this vital space. The positioning of these players depends upon the position of the ball. A free kick in the middle of the goal decreases the amount of space to be sealed off. (See Diagrams 14-6 and 14-7.) If an indirect free kick is awarded in the penalty area, as much of the goal as possible should be covered.

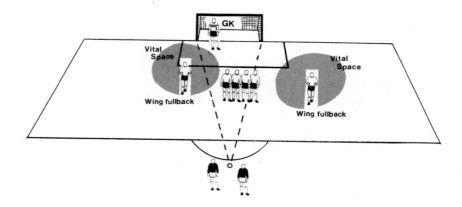

DIAGRAM 14-6

When there is less space to seal off, wing fullbacks are positioned wide of the wall to track down attacking players on the wings.

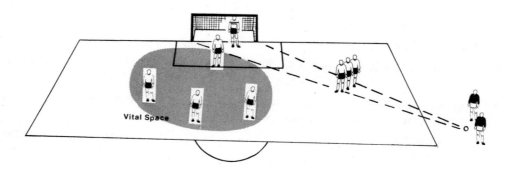

DIAGRAM 14-7

When there is more space to seal off, proficient headers of the ball are positioned in the vital space.

If the wall is positioned on the goal line all eleven players must stand between the goal posts. The goalkeeper then stands in the middle of the wall. Once the ball is touched, the entire wall attempts to smother the ball.

Throw-Ins

Defenders must retain their concentration and react promptly when the ball goes out of play. Any lapse in concentration at this time allows the opposition to take advantage of the lack of mental preparation by the defense.

Defending players must:

- Move quickly to mark players
- Move to mark players tightly, the closer they are to the ball

Defenders who are marking players down the wings should be prepared for the long throw over their heads. Many attacking teams play the ball in this manner. The long throw into the penalty area requires:

- An alertness from the goalkeeper in moving to destroy the play
- An awareness by the defenders of the vital space that has to be sealed off

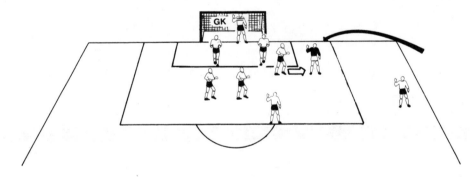

DIAGRAM 14-8

In defending against a long throw, the position of the attackers determines the defensive marking responsibilities.

Time is on the side of the defenders by allowing them to react to the ball. A long, driven throw can provide problems for the defense, especially if an attacker moves quickly to the ball in an attempt to flick the ball backward over the pursuing defender's head. On all throws it is important for all defenders to be concerned with concentrating and reacting. (See Diagram 14-8.)

Corner Kicks

It is again important that a defense respond quickly to the call by the referee that a corner kick has been awarded. The defense should position as follows:

- One defender covers the near post by positioning slightly outside of it. He must attack the space in front of him.
- One defender covers the back post by positioning inside of it and along the goal line.

- One defender stands 10 yards away from the ball to prevent the short corner kick and also to add a distraction.
- The goalkeeper stands along the goal line in the middle of the goal to balance the near-post and back-post corner kicks.
- The goalkeeper commands the penalty area by his verbal and physical presence.

The remaining defending players must then seal off other threatened areas:

- At the near post
- At the back post
- Beyond the six-yard line

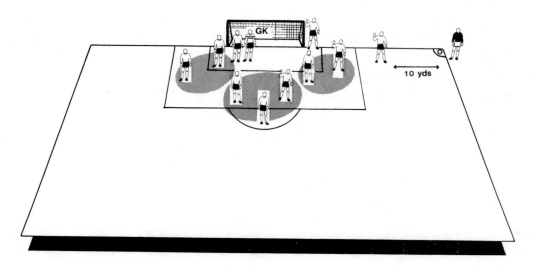

DIAGRAM 14-9
Defenders must first seal off the vital spaces before they begin to track down attacking players.

Defenders must seal off the vital spaces first, before they begin to track down players. (See Diagram 14-9.) A defender has sufficient time to adjust his position to the ball and the attacker. Attacking players will undoubtedly attempt to move into these vital spaces as the ball is being played. The defenders must attack the ball and not the player. A play is often destroyed by the quickness of a defensive player toward the ball. Being first to the ball achieves this.

Goal Kicks

All ten defenders are given time to adjust their positions. Each attacking player should be kept in view and marked by a defender. A balance should be achieved between:

- Giving an attacker too much room in which to work if he receives the ball
- Marking him so tightly that he can roll off into an open space

Once the goal kick has been taken the defender should:

- Move to intercept the ball
- Apply pressure on the player receiving the ball by preventing him from turning

Attacking at Set Plays

Tactical preplanning for handling a dead ball can be instrumental in making the attempted threat on goal, but only provided the plan remains relatively simple. Coaches and players who construct detailed set moves involving many players can lose their advantage of possession—complexity leads to confusion.

Free Kicks

The first priority at a free kick is to take it quickly. A direct free kick provides an immediate shooting opportunity. An indirect free kick provides an immediate shooting opportunity. An indirect free kick provides a second player a shooting opportunity. An alert offense can disrupt the concentration and preparation of a defense by:

- Obstructing the goalkeeper's vision
- Causing confusion for defenders in the wall
- Attacking the rebound by following up on the shot
- Positioning two players on the ball, introducing the element of surprise as to who will take the shot

All players involved with the free kick should combine their movements in an attempt to confuse the opposition. There are three groupings:

- Players on the ball
- Players in the wall
- Players around the wall

Players on the Ball

The two players taking the free kick must understand their responsibilities and execute soundly. Their movements into the ball require:

- Approaches from different angles.
- Approaches at different speeds.
- The correct timing to allow both players to be close to the ball when it is played. If there is too much distance and time between these two players, the decoy run will be wasted.

Players in the Wall

The remaining players involved in the wall must understand their responsibilities and execute soundly. Their positioning and movements should:

- Obstruct the goalkeeper's vision of the ball. This is achieved by standing in front of the wall on a line to the goalkeeper.
- Allow a more direct followup to any rebound off a shot.

Players Around the Wall

The remaining players around the wall must understand their responsibilities and execute soundly. Their involvement becomes more pronounced the wider the free kick is taken from goal. If a direct shot cannot be taken, these players are used as target players. The main threat on goal for a ball that is played into the penalty area is around the near post. Defenders set a wall to protect only this area of the goal. It is infrequent that defenders are placed behind it. This near-post area can be exploited in two ways:

- By the target players' moving into this area at the last moment
- By the decoy player's continuing his run around the wall and into the area

Attacking players can utilize this area only if they are first to the ball. (See Diagrams 14-10 and 14-11.)

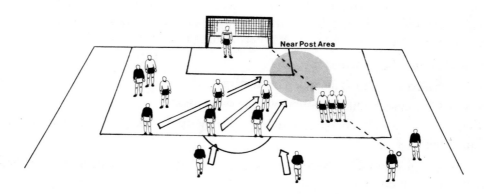

DIAGRAM 14-10
The offense plays the ball behind the wall and into the path of the target players. Not all the attackers move into this area. Some players will remain around the "D" to take advantage of any ball that is cleared.

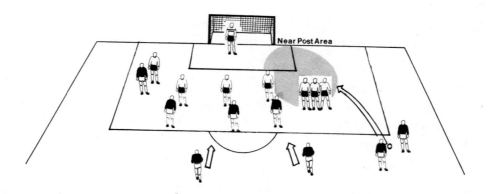

DIAGRAM 14-11
The decoy player attacks the unmarked area outside of the wall in his move to exploit the near-post area.

You can rarely predict what a defense will do in any given situation. Free kicks are no different. Keeping the play simple ensures that it is within each player's capabilities. It would be beneficial in the long run if you could limit your planning for free kicks to two areas: shooting, and passing and shooting.

Throw-Ins

As with free kicks, a throw-in should be taken quickly and played forward behind defenders. An alert defense marks tightly, and therefore attacking players must create space in order to utilize it. If an unmarked player is available, the ball should be played there first. This removes the need for combined movements and possible confusion. One of the most effective throw-in plays is the ball that is played down the wing into space. The combined movements and effort of two players can produce successful outcomes if their timing is correct. The movement of a tall target player can be effective for the long throw. The near-post area is best utilized by this player; if he can direct the ball over to the goal, this should be encouraged. If the throw is short, a run toward the ball can be glanced backward into the path of other attacking players.

Corner Kicks

When the ball has been played out for a corner kick, defenders are usually present in the immediate area of the goal, making it counterproductive to rush the corner kick. The offense should take the time to move into their predetermined positions.

Six-Yard Area

The primary area that the attacking team tries to penetrate is found in this small but productive area. From stationary positions, attacking players must create and then utilize this vital space. Four players are positioned in the six-yard area. (See Diagram 14-12.)

DIAGRAM 14-12
Attacking players move into and away from the six-yard area in an attempt to create and utilize vital space.

Player A moves toward the ball for a back header. Player B moves out from in front of the goalkeeper toward the six-yard line. Player C also moves out with the awareness that a ball may be backheaded into his path. Player D is used as the security player to cover any ball that is miskicked too far into the back post area.

Penalty Area

- *The Wave.* This refers to the group of players who move into the vital area from deep at the back of the penalty area by making staggered runs in an attempt to disrupt the marking responsibility of the defense. Two areas are attacked by the wave: the back post and the middle of the goal. Three players work in the wave from positions close to each other. By breaking away at different times and in different directions, they place the defense in a confused state. The players in the wave must have a clear understanding of their responsibilities once the wave begins to move. If the corner kick is planned for the back post, two of the three in the wave move toward the far post while the third moves into the middle. If the kick is intended for the middle or near post, two of the three push into the middle. The runs must be timed with the movements of the six-yard area players and the signal from the player taking the corner kick. If space is created by the six-yard area players, the wave can continue to utilize it.

- *The Near Post.* An additional attacker begins his run directly toward the near post from a position just inside the "D." The space created by the original near-post player's run toward the ball can be utilized quickly. The run must be timed with the movement of the original near-post player and the signal from the player taking the corner kick.

Outside the Penalty Area

- *The Garbage Player.* The area around the "D" is an area where partially cleared balls can be found. This loose garbage can be attacked by the player holding his position and evaluating the situation.

- *The Kicker.* A smooth action is required for a corner kick to reach the target areas. This player must work not only on the fundamentals of his kicking technique, but also on the timing of his run into the ball. The cue for attackers to begin their runs is given by a player who raises his hand and then drops it. Coordinating a run with the arm-drop requires practice until familiarity and good timing are established. (See Diagram 14-13.)

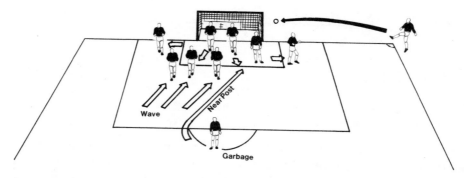

DIAGRAM 14-13

Wave, near-post, and garbage players move to their correct positions for a corner kick.

Goal Kicks

In playing the ball long and down the field a goalkeeper can feel he has performed his function of clearing the ball away from his own penalty area. This kind of thinking provides the opposition with an excellent chance to regain possession. Maintaining possession should be a priority for the goalkeeper, but to achieve this his teammates must provide sufficient constructive movement to receive a pass and take defenders away.

The offense can create space for both functions by spreading out from side to side and spreading out from end to end. (See Diagram 14-14.) Both wing fullbacks can have an immediate effect on the outcome of the goal kick by moving out wide toward the sidelines, close to the corner flag. One of two outcomes will follow:

- They are available to receive a short goal kick.
- The opposition follows them, allowing space to be created in the middle of the field.

Other attacking players must react to the situation by positioning themselves in advantageous areas of the field. Once the kick has been taken, these players now react to the placement of the ball and provide support as well as additional constructive runs to create space if possible.

A goalkeeper sometimes allows an outfield player to take the kick because of his own inability to kick the ball correctly. This indicates the need for more time and effort to be spent in practice on the weakness of the goalkeeper's distribution. Allowing an outfield player to take the goal kick provides a numerical advantage to the opposition, an advantage that cannot be afforded in such an important area of the field.

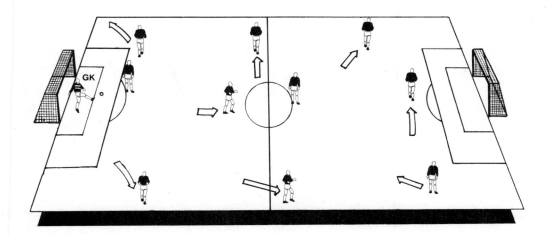

DIAGRAM 14-4
Attacking players spread side to side and end to end to create space for the offense to work in.

INDEX

Peter Loewer is an accomplished writer, photographer, and botanical illustrator who has authored over thirty books on gardening, native plants, and the natural sciences, including *The Evening Garden*, *The New Small Garden*, *Secrets of the Great Gardeners*, *Winter Gardening in the Southeast*, *Fragrant Gardens*, and *The Moonflower*, one of three children's books co-authored with his wife, Jean Jenkins. His popular *The Wild Gardener* was named by the American Horticulture Society as one of the seventy-five best gardening books of the twentieth century. Peter has also served as editor, art director, and a regular contributor for a variety of

publications, and has authored numerous articles for such magazines as *Green Scene*, *American Horticulturist*, *Organic Gardening*, and *Carolina Gardener*.

For over ten years he has hosted "The Wild Gardener" on WCQS, Asheville, North Carolina's, public broadcasting station, and been the lead commentator for the monthly garden show "Conversations." He is the owner of Graphos Studio of illustration and design and several of Peter's botanical drawings are in the permanent collection of the Hunt Institute for Botanical Documentation at Carnegie-Mellon University. Peter and his wife live and garden in Asheville, North Carolina.